What Were You Thinking?

*Interviewing Bible-Time Women in a
Modern-Day Classroom*

by Cheryl Elliott

What Were You Thinking?
Interviewing Bible-Time Women in a Modern-Day Classroom
by Cheryl Elliott

Printed in the United States of America

ISBN 978-1-60791-823-3

www.xulonpress.com

Contents

Acknowledgements

While this book may have begun quite by accident on my part, it was not a surprise to God, who had already placed a number of women in my life with smiling faces and calloused knees to serve as prayer warriors and special encouragers. Thank you, Father!

To my mother, Shirley Sandefur: Thank you for seeing my potential when I couldn't and for being my biggest fan and constant encourager. How blessed I am to have had you as an example of what a Christian woman is to be.

To my sister, Georgia Sharpe: Thank you for your patience in listening to these interviews over and over and over again, and for talking me through my many bouts of insecurity. How blessed I am to have you not only as a sister but also as a friend.

To my daughter, Stasie Holder: Thank you for your daily phone calls and for crying with me the morning I had to leave little Samuel with Eli. You are an amazing young woman. Thank you for thinking your mom can do anything!

To Tia, Judy, April, Maxine, Deborah, Georgia, Mary E., Janice, Karen, Mary B., Stasie, and Nancy: Each of you so graciously took on the role of one of these women and helped me bring her to life in our classroom. Thank you for your participation.

To my Sisters of Lazarus Sunday School Class: Thank you for your kind words of encouragement to me, not only in my first attempt at writing something of this nature but in teaching as well. Thank you for urging me to pursue publishing these interviews. Without your gentle shoves, these may still be under cover of darkness, tucked away in the back of a desk drawer.

To my copyeditor, Marcia Ford: Thank you for the time and energy you put into polishing the rough edges of my manuscript. Thank you for taking this first-timer by the hand, guiding her, and encouraging her to pursue a newly discovered gift.

In Loving Memory

Of my husband, Gary, my tireless sounding board
during the initial rough drafts

Foreword

I believe that the study of Scripture should be fresh and exciting—never boring! I also believe that we modern-day women are a lot more like Bible-time women than we realize. It is for these two reasons that these interviews got their start.

It is my prayer that as you "sit down and visit" with each one of these ladies, you will come away with a better understanding of not only her life in general but also her heart in particular. Realize, too, that I've taken a lot of liberty in writing these interviews, and with my own imagination I've filled in the blanks about how each of these Bible-time women thought and felt. My ultimate goal was to take these women away from the black-and-white sketches of the past and bring them into full-color, life-sized portraits in the present.

May God bless you as you personally get to know these women of the Bible.

Cheryl

Eve

Background Reading: Genesis 2:15–4:26
In-Class Reading: Genesis 2:15–4:8, 25
Key Verses: Genesis 3:6, 20-21

Interviewer: Eve, thank you for joining us this morning. We have been so anxious and excited to meet you. Of all the women we read about in the Bible, you're the one with the most remarkable beginning! Not only did you just wake up one day existing, but you were already an adult—and married! In the Bible we read that Adam was ecstatic when he first saw you. Were you just as excited to see him? What were your thoughts when God first introduced you to Adam?

Eve: You know, when I was listening to the Scriptures about my life, they brought back a lot of memories—both good and bad. I was a bit surprised to hear Adam's reaction when he saw me for the first time. I guess, in the course of living, I had forgotten his initial excitement. Oh, I was very pleased with Adam as well. He was absolutely perfect—tall, dark, handsome—and strong! It was when I first laid eyes on him that I realized the beating of my own heart. Sounds mushy, I know, but we were so much in love!

We were literally made for each other. We would spend hours just walking the Garden, hand-in-hand, talking, laughing at the antics of the animals, smelling the flowers, enjoying the gentle breezes. It was an absolute paradise. Everything was just perfect. It all seems like a dream now . . . it was so long ago.

Interviewer: Speaking of paradise, Eve, what was that like? What was it like to take a walk with God and talk with him whenever you wanted? Did you miss that once you moved?

Eve: Oh, it was so wonderful. God talked with us all the time—morning, noon, and night. I remember in the mornings God was always so eager to get the day started. Then, at noon, we would all just sit down, relax among the flowers and trees, and just listen to the birds sing. But I think his favorite part of the day was our evening strolls together—I know they were mine. God truly looked forward to the evening walks he took with us. He always asked us about our day—what new discoveries we had made, what had caused us to laugh. He would laugh along with us and was delighted with each and every new discovery. I can still hear his laugh the day we told him about the smell of the skunk! He laughed so hard! That got Adam and me to laughing, too. We all laughed so much that there were tears running down our faces!

But you know, that was typical of God. He was so much fun to be with, and he was interested in absolutely everything we did. And he was always so excited to point out parts of his creation to us as we wandered through the Garden—almost as if he couldn't wait for us to see them and enjoy them for ourselves!

And yes, when we first left, I missed his closeness and his genuine concern for us; his laughter, the twinkle in his eye. But then I discovered that no matter where I was, I could talk with him, and he would talk with me. I soon realized that even though distance may have separated us, God was big enough to bridge that gap—and he never once failed to do so. He was just as close to me and just as concerned about me after I left the Garden as he always had been.

Interviewer: You know, we find that's true even today—when we allow him and take the time to be with him. But let's step back for a moment to that day in the Garden—you know which one I'm talking about. Eve, what were you thinking?

Eve: Obviously, I wasn't thinking! That serpent—oh, he made me so mad!—that serpent downright lied to me. Before that time, I never even knew what a lie was! He was such a smooth talker. I kept telling him what God had said, but he always seemed to have an explanation. Not having the experience of a childhood, I was totally unprepared to argue with him. After all, I had never argued a day in my life! I didn't even know what arguing was back then!

Anyway, the serpent told me such wonderful things about the fruit from that tree—how it tasted so good, better than any other fruit; how it would enrich my life, allowing me know as much as God; and how it would make me wise, just like God. For a while, the serpent had me so focused on the things I didn't have that I couldn't see the countless good things I did have. I began to resent God for holding out on me. Eventually . . . well, I just couldn't resist.

It just sounded so wonderful—and I certainly didn't want to be left out! Then I began to justify what I was about to do. I thought what a nice surprise it would be for God to have someone to talk to who was on the same intellectual level as he was. Now I feel like such an idiot.

Interviewer: Now Eve, honey, don't go beating yourself up. We all find ourselves in similar situations even today. We are bombarded all the time with slick salesmen trying to convince us that their product will cure whatever is bothering us. If we want to lose a few pounds, there's a pill that will just cause them to "melt away." If we're short of cash, there's this little card from which we can "magically" get money. There are all kinds of temptations out there. And with every single one we, too, try to justify ahead of time why we should go ahead and give in. Given the same circumstances you had, we would probably have done the exact same thing you did. You know, we have a saying nowadays, "If it sounds too good to be true, it probably is!" Even today, Satan continues to be the slickest salesman of all.

Oh, I'm sorry about that, Eve. I'm beginning to get a bit sidetracked. I guess you can tell what a hot topic slick salesmen are even in our modern-day world! Enough about us—let's get back to you. Please, continue on—tell us, what happened after you tasted the fruit?

Eve: Well, you know, it did taste as good as the serpent had said. I don't know if I'd call it the best, but it certainly was good—and nothing bad seemed to happen right then, so I took it to Adam. Just like me, he was a bit hesitant. But I convinced him to try it—

he would like it! I understand you use that saying a lot, too. Anyway, I think that's when it first dawned on me that I was different. Here I was, standing in the Garden, trying to convince Adam to eat the forbidden fruit. I was acting like that serpent! For a brief moment, I thought about stopping Adam, but I was too ashamed to admit my mistake. Then, after he ate, we both immediately had this sudden change come over us. We knew we would never be the same. We began to see each other differently—and we didn't like what we saw or felt. It was awful.

Interviewer: What did you do then?

Eve: Well, we did what we thought we had to—we figured out a way to cover ourselves up! We did it so quietly and secretly. I'm not sure why. I'm sure we both knew that God would find out sooner or later. Can you even begin to understand?

Interviewer: Understand what? Quietly and secretly covering up sin? Are you kidding? It seems that as the years go by, we humans get better and better at it—we do it more and more often. But as Christians, we don't believe that God will find out sooner or later. Rather, we know that he already knows! Yet, we still have a tendency to want to think that if we ignore it, or hide it, or do it in secret, that everything will be OK. Of course, you and I both know that's not going to happen. We have to ask God to forgive us and swallow our pride and accept God's punishment. Did God punish you for disobeying him?

Eve: Well, God was very angry. It took him a while to get us to be 100 percent truthful with him and tell the whole story about what had happened and whose fault it was. Adam blamed me; I blamed the serpent. The serpent insisted that he didn't force me—he only "suggested" I eat the fruit. It was really quite uncomfortable. We were wrong, and we knew it. But none of us wanted to admit it.

When God finally got us to tell the whole truth, he punished us in different ways. He cursed the serpent and caused him to grovel in the dust, crawling on his belly. For me, he said that when I began to have children of my own, it would be extremely painful. God told Adam that he would have to work hard to provide for himself and his family. God was not a happy camper—and neither were we at that point. But you know what God did? Right in the middle of his dishing out punishment, he stopped and made clothes for us. Evidently he didn't think the fig leaves provided enough coverage! Instead, he killed an innocent animal and made clothes for us from its skin. We were so ashamed and so humbled. To think that an animal had to die because of us! You probably don't know what I mean, but it brought me to tears.

Interviewer: Eve, I think we know exactly how you felt. Thousands of years after you lived, God did much the same for us. We humans are such sinners that there's no way for us to save ourselves, so he sent his Son, Jesus Christ, to this world to save us—to cover our sins. After a few short years of living among us, Jesus willingly died so we could be saved. We had become so sinful that there was no way we could find salvation on our own. It took Jesus Christ and His blood. Talk about being humbled! We fall face down on the floor in tears every time this realization of His sacrifice truly hits us.

You said earlier that God paused in the middle of your punishment to make you clothes. How else did he punish you?

Eve: Oh, it was awful! Even now, it's hard to talk about. He banished us from the Garden of Eden. That's the only home we had ever known. And at that time, we weren't sure if we'd ever see or talk with God again. We really had become friends, you know. That's why I know his heart was breaking, too. I think he also knew what was ahead for us, and that caused him even more heartbreak.

Interviewer: What was ahead for you?

Eve: Well, it's kind of a long story. We got settled, and Adam began to grow food for us and tend the animals. He worked so hard! Day after day he was out there trying his best to provide for us. Meanwhile, I became pregnant. When I gave birth to Cain, that's when I understood how severe God's punishment was for me. Oh, you talk about excruciating pain! Well, it wasn't too long until I also gave birth to Abel, and for a time, life seemed to run pretty smoothly. Oh, we had our ups and downs, mind you. Being close in age, some days the boys would play together as best friends and other days, well, worst enemies! Sometimes I wanted to pull my hair out in frustration. I may not have known about arguing when I encountered the serpent, but my boys seemed to learn it naturally. And being their mother, I had to learn what you call child psychology as I went along. But they did grow up to become handsome young men—even if I say so myself!

You know, Cain became a great farmer. He had what you would call a "green thumb." Everything just seemed to grow for him. And Abel, well, Abel had a knack with animals. Some would follow him around wherever he went. He always seemed to have them by his side, talking to them, petting them. Oh, how he loved his animals!

I remember as clearly as if it were yesterday the second most horrible day of my life. My sons were going through an unusually rugged time of competition between them. You know how they do—who's fastest, who's strongest, who's smartest. With them, everything was a competition.

From the time the boys were little, we had told them about God and the Garden of Eden. Adam and I regularly brought gifts to God, asking for his forgiveness and thanking him for continuing to be with us and providing for us. We knew from our days in the Garden that God was in control and everything belonged to him. Giving back to him a small portion of what he'd given us wasn't too much to ask— especially after what we had done. In fact, we were thankful to be able to do it—to ask God's forgiveness and favor. And we did it over and over again. We didn't want anything to ever come between us and God again. We tried to teach that to the boys and explain to them how it's not the gift, or even the size of the gift, that matters. What matters is the attitude of your heart—that when you give back to God, what's important is that you're giving because you want to give and that you wish you could give more. There's so much wrapped up in our attitude toward God when it comes to giving and pleading with him for his forgiveness and mercy.

Interviewer: Eve, I know that it must be painful, but could you tell us about that day? What went wrong?

Eve: Well, you know, with children you don't always get the whole story. You just kind of piece together information and draw your own conclusions. I'm not sure who first suggested that they go and offer a sacrifice to God—and it really doesn't matter. But I think Cain may have looked at this as just another big competition. I think Cain saw this as a "let's see who God likes best" opportunity, whereas Abel was giving as he always had—from his heart. I truly believe both boys gave the best of what they had—Abel of his animals and Cain of the best crops he had grown. But I don't think Cain's heart was right or that he gave out of a pure motivation.

Perhaps he was not truly repentant. I think that's why Abel's offering was accepted and Cain's wasn't. God even gave Cain a chance for a "do-over," but he was too angry.

Interviewer: How did you find out about what had happened?

Eve: At first, we didn't know. All we knew was that Cain had become angrier and more quick-tempered than he ever had been. Yet he also seemed sadder, quieter—almost as if he had something he couldn't get off his mind, but he didn't want to share. This went on for several days, and both Adam and I tried to talk with him, but he just shut us out. Actually, it was Abel who finally told us about the sacrifices and what had happened.

Interviewer: Once you heard about the sacrifice incident, what did you do? Did you approach Cain with what you had found out?

Eve: That's exactly what we did! We thought that if he knew that we knew the whole story, he would open up to us—share what he was feeling—and he would let us help him.

Interviewer: Did he?

Eve: No. Instead, he only seemed to get angrier and more withdrawn. Now he was angry not only at God but also at Abel because he tattled on him. I think he saw himself as a failure in God's sight, in Abel's sight, and now in our sight. We weren't sure what to do. I guess we thought he would eventually come around. But things only got worse.

Interviewer: Oh, Eve, are you sure you're up to talking about this? I know this must be terribly difficult for you. Do you need to take a break?

Eve: It's hard all right. But I'll be fine. Let me go ahead and share what happened.

Everything came to a head one afternoon when the boys were out in the field together. We initially took that as a good sign—that Cain was coming around and the two of them were becoming friends again. Little did we know that we would never again see them, touch them, hug them, laugh with them, talk with them. The last we saw, they were walking off into the field together.

We didn't know that people could die like that. We had seen animals die and we had sacrificed animals ourselves, but we just didn't translate that to people. God had told us that our days would be numbered, but we really didn't understand what that meant! How could someone so young die? Why? And how could Cain have killed his own flesh and blood? What good could ever come of that?

Interviewer: Did you ever get your questions answered?

Eve: Not really. Not then. Ultimately Adam and I had to trust God. There was really nothing else we could do. Not only did we lose Abel that day, but we lost Cain as well. I also learned that the pain of childbirth isn't just at birth—it's with you the rest of your life as you watch your children make—and hopefully learn from—their mistakes, or when they're sick or injured. Your intense, painful love for them lasts a lifetime.

Interviewer: Well said. Eve, I am so sorry, but we're going to have to wrap this up pretty soon. Could you briefly tell us "the rest of the story"? How did you continue on?

Eve: Well, as you can guess, it wasn't easy. I missed those two boys terribly. For a time, I felt lost. I had been a mother to those two for so long. Now it was back to just Adam and me. I had to re-learn how to cook for only two people and find ways to fill my time. But God was faithful. He never did desert us. He blessed Adam and me with many more children. We named the first one "Seth," which means "granted." God had granted us another son, and we were so happy. God truly can turn your sorrow into joy!

Interviewer: Eve, thank you so much for joining us today. You led such a remarkable life. And even though it was painful at times, we appreciate your sharing with us. In closing, could you sum up two or three important lessons in your life that you would like women of today to learn?

Eve: Well, first, I would say to learn to be content. Lack of contentment was the underlying reason Adam and I were kicked out of the Garden of Eden. Learn to be happy with what God gives you—or doesn't give you.

Second, love those around you. Never take for granted the children God has entrusted to you. It doesn't matter if they're your own or someone else's—love them, nurture them, teach them about God. They can't get too much teaching!

Third, but certainly no less important, I'd say become aware of how Satan tries to work in your life. For Adam and me, he first came disguised as a serpent. For Cain and Abel, I think he came disguised as competition. You can never be too careful. We lived the rest of our lives with the painful consequences of our actions that day in the Garden of Eden. But if we let them, those same consequences can teach us and remind us of lessons we've had to learn the hard way. Learn to listen to your gut feeling. Satan will come at you in different forms and in different ways. He is a master of disguise and is a quick-change artist. If you sense something is wrong, then it probably is.

Interviewer: Thank you, Eve. It has been such a pleasure visiting with you today. You have been such a blessing to us. Thank you for sharing from your heart.

DISCUSSION QUESTIONS:

1. Since Eve began life as an adult, when she first encountered Satan, she didn't know or recognize what a lie was or how to argue with Satan. What are some other childhood experiences we all go through that help prepare us for adulthood?

2. Eve justified her tasting of the fruit by thinking that it would be nice for God to have someone on his intellectual level to talk to. In what ways do we justify our sinful actions? How do we try to cover up sin?

3. In the interview, Satan is described as both a "slick salesman" and a "quick-change artist." What are some other ways he could be described?

4. Eve mentions a couple of ways Satan disguised himself—in the form of a serpent and in the form of unhealthy competition. Under what kinds of disguises have you seen Satan come into your life or the lives of others?

5. Eve said that the lack of contentment is what ultimately caused Adam and her to sin, and she urges us to be happy with our circumstances. Why do you think contentment is such a hard thing to achieve?

6. Now that we've met Eve "face-to-face" and heard her side of the story, with which part of Eve's story can you most closely identify?

Abigail

Background Reading: 1 Samuel 25:1-42
In-Class Reading: 1 Samuel 25:1-42
Key Verses: 1 Samuel 25:32-33

Interviewer: Welcome, Abigail. It's good to have you here with us today. Before we begin this interview, I need to let you know that I really didn't know a whole lot about you or your story. It wasn't until I began to prepare for our one-on-one time together that I really began to see how truly remarkable you were. To begin, why don't you tell us a little about yourself?

Abigail: Oh, goodness, there's really not that much to tell. I find it hard to believe that the Scriptures said I was pretty, smart, and wise. I never felt that way at all. Actually, I always considered myself an average woman. For a long time, the only way I felt I stood out was because I just happened to marry into wealth.

Interviewer: Well, all we read about you is good. In fact, women throughout the ages have named their own daughters "Abigail"—some because of you. If you wouldn't mind, would you begin by telling us about your first husband, Nabal?

Abigail: You know, in my day, we attached a lot of meanings to names. And for the most part, they seemed to fit our personalities as we got older. Nabal's name meant "fool," and he was every bit the fool in a lot of ways. He may have been rich, but he was one really bad man, which caused me some hardship and heartache. He was, among other things, rude, dishonest, self-centered, and hot-tempered. He had a tendency to use people when it profited him. But if they should need help or ask a favor of him, he turned his back on them every time.

Interviewer: Yet you married him. I assumed you loved him?

Abigail: No, I never did actually. Back then, men and women didn't often marry for love. Usually it was for just about every reason except love. For Nabal and me, well, he just wanted someone to cater to his wants and needs. When he chose me, I really didn't have a say in the matter. It was decided for me—an arranged marriage, so to speak.

Interviewer: How did you feel about that?

Abigail: Well, at first I wasn't too upset. After all, Nabal was wealthy, and I figured I'd at least be well taken care of. And who knows? Maybe we would learn to love each other as we spent more time together. But as time went on, and I began to see him as he really was, I became more and more disillusioned. Since we had no children for me to take care of, and servants took care of me, my life really became rather boring. I actually longed for the day that a little excitement would come into my life—anything! I didn't care what. I just wanted a day when I could feel alive again. Useful. Needed. Do you know what I mean?

Interviewer: Yes, I think I do. Today's modern woman calls it "getting into a rut." Our lives today are perhaps as busy as yours was boring. We often long for a change of pace. We do the same things over and over. We get up, feed and dress the kids, kiss everyone goodbye, go to work, come home, kiss the husband, feed and re-dress the kids for soccer practice, sit at the soccer field, come back home, feed the kids again, throw dishes into the dishwasher, give the kids baths, do a load of laundry, kiss the husband, go to bed, get up, and do it all over again the next day. Even single women can find themselves in ruts of their own. Occasionally, we might even throw in a little bit of Bible reading and prayer. But it's basically the same routine day in, day out. Some of us actually long for a "boring" day like you described— one where we could take time for a long, hot, soaking bubble bath. A day we could curl up on the sofa and read a book without feeling guilty. A day all to ourselves—peaceful, quiet.

Well, moving on. I happen to know you did get your wish. Some excitement did come into your life. Would you mind telling us about that?

Abigail: Remember when I said Nabal used people? Well, that's how it all started. Several weeks earlier, my husband had been out in the fields with our herd and shepherds when trouble came. It happened that David and his men were in nearby fields, and they rushed to Nabal's aid—protecting him, his herd, his servants—his entire wealth, which, to Nabal, was everything. During the time David and his men protected Nabal's flocks, nothing Nabal owned was lost or stolen. Absolutely nothing! Nabal returned home with everything he had taken, which probably would not have been the case had David and his men not been around. I'm certain Nabal thanked David at the time. And I'm just as certain it was *not* heart-felt—it was just the polite thing for him to do. Then they went their separate ways.

Well, fast-forward a few weeks, and now the sandal's on the other foot—David needed Nabal's help. Little did David know what kind of man Nabal actually was. But he was soon to find out. You would think that a man who apparently had it all would be more gracious, more considerate. Oh, but not Nabal. He embarrassed me more times than I could count.

Interviewer: Was Nabal really all that bad? You sound a bit harsh. Surely he had some good qualities.

Abigail: Nope. None. Believe me, I had plenty of time on my hands to try to find them, too! He cared for no one except himself.

Interviewer: You said earlier that David came looking for Nabal's help. What was it that David needed?

Abigail: Well, all this time, David and his men had been wandering out in those same fields, waiting for Saul to cool down—but that's another story for another day! Anyway, now David and his men were beginning to run short of food, water, and other supplies. So, David sent messengers to Nabal to ask for help.

Granted, David was asking for supplies for several hundred men. But Nabal was actually so wealthy that giving up that amount of provisions would hardly have been noticeable. It would have made only a small dent in what he had—a drop in the bucket, so to speak. But instead of helping them, Nabal was extremely rude to them. Here was the chance for Nabal to return a huge favor in a small way. Instead, he became hostile toward David's messengers. He even acted as if he didn't know who David was and all but accused the messengers of being renegade outlaws! Even the servant who came running to tell me what had happened was appalled. He said it was the worst treatment he had ever seen, and he actually feared that the messengers would return with David and bring harm to Nabal and maybe even his estate.

Interviewer: Where were you during all this?

Abigail: Actually, this happened during sheep-shearing time, which meant this was cause for a great celebration. And if there's one thing Nabal knew how to do, it was party! There was food and drink in abundance. Everyone from all around had been invited to the festivities, so we had a lot of people around our property. How I wish I had been with Nabal the moment David's messengers came. But as it turned out, I was entertaining the women at the time. Had I been there, maybe I could have talked to Nabal and gotten him to see how wrong he was. But honestly, I don't know that I would have made much of a difference. Nabal wasn't used to listening to anyone else—only to his own voice and the thoughts in his own big, self-centered head.

Interviewer: What happened next?

Abigail: Well, David's messengers went back to camp empty-handed and told David what Nabal had said and how badly they had been treated.

Interviewer: I'll bet that didn't sit well with David!

Abigail: Oh, you bet it didn't! David wasn't a man to let something like this go either. After all, David himself was well-known and well-respected. We all knew David was going to be king someday, which made it all the more shocking how Nabal treated David's messengers.

Interviewer: What did you do when you learned what Nabal had done—or not done—in this case?

Abigail: Well, I lost no time! Thanks to the festivities already in full swing, I had ready access to all kinds of supplies. So, I had my servant girls help me gather up 200 loaves of bread and a whole bunch of other things, like wine, sheep, grain, and cakes—anything and everything I could think of. We loaded down the donkeys and set out ourselves to find David and try to make amends.

Interviewer: Did Nabal know what you were up to?

Abigail: Goodness, no! I had learned that sometimes it was best to confront him after the fact. If I had told him what I had planned, I'm sure he would have stopped me. No, this time I decided to take matters into my own hands.

Interviewer: Did you find David?

Abigail: Oh, yes, we found him all right! I was riding my donkey down into a ravine (which, by the way, is easier said than done) when I saw David and his men coming toward me. They nearly scared me to death, there were so many of them! And by the way they moved, you could certainly tell they were on a "mission." Here I was, slowly plodding along, trying to keep my balance on the donkey, and here they were, hundreds of them, marching straight at me, armed to kill. They literally took up the entire path!

Interviewer: What did you do? How were you able to get out of their way?

Abigail: Actually, I didn't get out of their way. Believe it or not, I did just the opposite. I took a deep breath, got off my donkey, and fell face down on the ground before David.

Interviewer: You did what? Abigail, what in the world were you thinking? You could have been trampled to death!

Abigail: You know, at that point I was just going on pure adrenaline and reacting the best I knew how at the moment. I was willing to try anything I could to make right Nabal's terrible wrong. I had already rehearsed in my mind what I would say to David at least a hundred times. I just hadn't expected to run into David so soon. I guess I thought I'd find him out in the fields. So when I ran into him, even though it was on a narrow path leading down into a ravine, I just did what I felt I had to do and didn't worry about the consequences.

Interviewer: What happened next?

Abigail: Well, here I was, lying face down in the dirt, covered in dust from head to toe. I'm sure I was not a pretty sight then! And come to think of it, I probably didn't look too smart, either!

Anyway, at the time, my appearance was the least of my worries. I remember I was shaking so hard. I was terrified to even look at David. After all, I was Nabal's wife—the wife of the man with whom he was so infuriated! I had no idea how David would respond to me or to what I was about to say.

So, before I even dared look at him, I begged him to let me take all the blame for Nabal's actions and to reconsider what he intended to do to Nabal. Then, still trembling with fear, I began kind of inching my way up to my knees, all the time appealing to David's character—and his relationship with the Lord. I reminded him that revenge should be left to God and that he shouldn't pursue bloodshed as a way to avenge himself—that he didn't want something like that hanging over his head when he became king.

Interviewer: How did David react to that?

Abigail: Well, he accepted my offering and my apology. Then he leaned down and helped me to my feet and blessed me! I was stunned! He actually thanked me for preventing him from taking matters into his own hands. He realized that seeking his own revenge would not have satisfied him—not really. Deep down, he knew that the peace he was looking for in this situation could only be found in God. That's also when David told me the extent of what he had planned—to kill not only Nabal but also all the men of our household by the next morning.

Interviewer: Wow! It's a good thing you acted so quickly. How did you know what to say to David or how to approach him?

Abigail: I didn't know. All I knew was that it had to be done. I knew David was a God-fearing man, so I reminded him of that. And from that point on, I was trusting God for what to say the entire time. At the end of my speech, I even asked David to remember me when he became successful and became king! Can you believe I was so bold as to ask such a thing? Me—a woman! A nobody! By the time David became king, he would have a whole lot more on his mind than trying to remember one woman! I was so embarrassed at blurting out such a remark that my face immediately turned beet red. To this day, I can't believe I said such a thing!

Interviewer: Sometimes—too many times, actually—I seem to do much the same thing. It's that last sentence or phrase I want to beat myself up over. I've often wondered why I couldn't have stopped while I was ahead—when I at least sounded credible! But no, not me. It seems I keep talking until I make a fool of myself. Then, that's all I can think about, which compounds the embarrassment.

So, you've just prevented a deadly disaster. What next? Did you have your fill of excitement, or was there more to come?

Abigail: Well, yes to both! That could certainly have been enough excitement to last me a long time! But sadly, there was still more ahead for me. I'll get to that in a minute.

First, I knew I had to tell Nabal everything. So, just as I had done with David, I spent the trip home rehearsing in my mind how I would go about doing that. I knew it wouldn't be easy and that he would be furious with me for what I had done. I prayed that he would see how it was the best thing to do under the circumstances. I knew that I had to tell him immediately. I saw no point in dragging it out, and besides, he may have realized that I, and some of my servant girls, hadn't been around all day.

But when I got home, I found that he apparently hadn't missed me at all and instead was still in the midst of partying. By now he had gotten very, very drunk. Seeing what was going on made me even madder about what he had done to David and his men! You know, what really ticked me off is that he probably spent more of his precious wealth on that drunken party of his than he would have if he'd just given the supplies to David in the first place! Nabal's priorities were so screwed up. Anyway, I now had to wait until the next morning, after he was sober, to tell him. And let me tell you, confronting him and talking to him was almost as hard—if not harder—than the prospect of talking to David had been.

Interviewer: How so?

Abigail: Well, we women were taught—and expected— to revere our husbands. I had to be extremely careful how I went about telling Nabal so he wouldn't think I was being disrespectful. I wanted him to see that I only did what was in his best interest. Believe me, the entire time I was talking to him, I felt as if I was walking on eggshells. I knew that everything I said had to be worded just right. But I also wanted him to realize the seriousness of what he had done and the danger he had put not only himself in but his innocent servants as well. My greatest desire was that he would begin to change.

Interviewer: Did he?

Abigail: No. And that's the sad part. He really didn't get that chance. Remember when I said to David that revenge should be left up to God? Well, God chose that exact moment to start seeking revenge on David's behalf. The moment Nabal fully realized the seriousness of the situation and how close he had come to losing it all, his heart began to give out, and he died just 10 days later. A lot of good his wealth did him then!

Interviewer: Oh, Abigail, how awful that must have been for you. What did you do next?

Abigail: Well, Nabal's death was sudden—and yes, it was awful. But I really can't say I mourned for him a great deal. Remember, we had a loveless marriage. I mostly just felt sorry for him. His life—and mine—could have been a whole lot better if only Nabal hadn't been so self-absorbed.

You know, it's rather ironic, but as it turned out, it was shortly after Nabal died that I began to live!

Interviewer: What do you mean by that?

Abigail: Well, it really all happened so suddenly. And I was probably the most surprised and shocked person of all. Just after Nabal's death, David's messengers once again came calling at my home—this time they specifically asked for me! David had heard about Nabal's death, and he had wasted no time in sending for me, asking me to marry him.

Interviewer: What did you do? Did you? Marry him, that is?

Abigail: You bet I did! As soon as I learned that the messengers were there for me, once again I found myself face-down in the dirt. I was so humbled that this man of God hadn't remembered my seemingly foolish "last words" but instead had found me wise—and beautiful, even covered in dirt!

Interviewer: My goodness—how romantic! And what a turn of events!

Abigail: Well, it wasn't all romance, but it was pretty wonderful compared to my life with Nabal. Remember, David and his men were still on the run from Saul at that time. So my first days as David's wife were quite different from what I'd been accustomed to.

But life did settle down for me. And David did become king. And we did have children. Finally my life felt complete. I was no longer lonely and bored, but I was busy and happy. What more could a girl ask for?

Interviewer: Abigail, you have been such a joy to visit with today. I'm afraid our time is almost gone, and we need to wrap this up. But before I let you go, do you have some words of advice for women of today? What lessons did you learn that we would do well to learn?

Abigail: Well, first I'd say to be careful what you ask for—God just might give it to you. He brought a whole lot more excitement into my life than I ever dreamed. Not that I regret any part of it or how things turned out, but it was rather stressful at the time.

Then, I'd urge you all to remember that no matter how right you think you are, always be willing to stop and listen to the advice of others. David was always so thankful that he had taken the time to hear me out that day on the path. What took just a few short minutes saved him from a lifetime of regret.

Lastly, I'd say to trust God. When you're deeply concerned about someone or some situation, go to God. Talk to him. Let him guide your actions. Even when you're not sure of the outcome or the consequences, if you're trusting God completely, then you know everything will be OK in the end.

Interviewer: Abigail, again, thank you for visiting with us. After talking with you, I think the authors of the Scriptures were right—you are a beautiful, smart, and wise woman. You are an intelligent and resourceful woman who dared to do the right things. Thank you so much.

DISCUSSION QUESTIONS:

1. Abigail used a lot of negative adjectives to describe Nabal. Why do you think she did that, and was she justified?

2. Nabal was so rich that giving up provisions for David and his men would have hardly made a dent in his wealth. It seems his entire life was consumed with the things he had rather than the people around him. Even today, it sometimes seems that the richer people are, the stingier they tend to be. Why do you think that is?

3. When Abigail first speaks to David, one of the first things she requests is that David put all the blame for Nabal's actions on her. How hard do you think that was for her? How would you have defended your husband had you been wearing Abigail's shoes?

4. Abigail was embarrassed at her closing remarks, asking David to remember her when he became successful and was crowned king. If Abigail had been trusting God for what to say, why do you think she thought her parting words were "off script"? Knowing the end of the story, what do you think David thought about those last remarks?

5. Abigail urges us to be careful what we ask for—we just might get it. What examples in your life bear out the truth of that statement?

6. When we are wronged, our first reaction may not be as David's, which was to plan to murder the offender— at least, I hope not! How do we tend to react instead?

How hard is it to listen to (and act on) advice that is the opposite of what we want to hear?

Sapphira

Background Reading: Acts 2:1–5:11
In-Class Reading: Acts 2:1-6, 12-16, 41-47;
    4:32-5:11
Key Verses: Acts 5:7-8

Interviewer: Good morning, Sapphira. We have been so anxious to meet you.

Sapphira: Thank you. I must admit, though, that I nearly backed out and didn't come this morning. I wasn't exactly the picture-perfect Christian, and I know that my legacy throughout history has been more negative than positive. But I wanted the chance to tell you my side of the story—there's a lot more to it than others realize, you know!

Interviewer: Sapphira, that's exactly why we've asked you to come—so you could tell us your story in your own words. All we've ever known about you has been from Luke's perspective. First of all, could you begin by telling us just a little bit about yourself?

Sapphira: Well, Ananias and I were really just a typical couple and up-and-coming members of the church.

We weren't young—but young enough! The church was just in its infancy stage, which was a very exciting time for us. To be a part of all that was happening was absolutely incredible!

Interviewer: What exactly was happening?

Sapphira: Well, not too long after Jesus' death and resurrection—actually less than a couple of months—those of us who had been believers were having one of our usual early-morning prayer meetings when suddenly, all kinds of strange things began to happen. We heard a thunder-type sound that was louder than anything we'd ever heard before. Then, the next thing we knew, flames of fire began to settle on everyone in the room. Yet no one was getting burned. We didn't know what was happening! It was frightening yet exciting at the same time.

We soon learned that the noise wasn't just isolated to the room we were in. Because before we knew it, people came running from all over town to find out what was going on. At the time we hadn't realized it was the Holy Spirit who had come. In our excitement, we were all talking in languages we didn't even know or understand! But as it turned out, they "happened" to be the languages of all the people who had gathered. There wasn't a single person there who didn't understand what was being said. But you know what? Even though we were all seeing, hearing, and experiencing the exact same thing, there were two completely different versions as to what was happening.

Interviewer: What do you mean?

Sapphira: Well, some who heard us, even though they were as confused and amazed as we were, marveled at all that was going on; others outright accused us of being drunkards and out of control. That was a little hard for me to take. I would never think of doing such a thing! What did they think I was anyway? But honestly, in their defense, things were a bit chaotic.

Interviewer: I can understand how that could be a problem. When you talk about people speaking in all kinds of languages, what were you saying? And even though the people understood, did the words you were speaking make any sense to them?

Sapphira: When people stopped to listen, we made perfect sense to them. We were actually spontaneously praising God and shouting out all the wonderful things he had done for us. Nothing had been planned ahead of time—it just happened. When Ananias and I left the house that morning, we thought we were headed to our usual, quiet, meditative prayer meeting. As it turned out, we experienced "holy chaos." Thank goodness for Peter's quick thinking!

Interviewer: Why? What did Peter do?

Sapphira: Well, Peter took control of the situation—he, along with some of the other apostles. After getting things to quiet down a bit, Peter began preaching. Actually, I thought it turned out to be one of the best sermons I'd ever heard him preach! He preached for quite a long time, too! But no one seemed to mind. When it was all said and done, there were about 3,000 more believers who were baptized and added to the church that day. Talk about a revival!

Interviewer: It certainly was! I can't imagine that many new Christians all in one day in one place. How did your church handle that many new converts all at once? Surely these new believers needed more teaching and instruction in addition to that first sermon of Peter's that they heard. I cannot begin to imagine how a church would go about helping that many people to grow and mature in their faith all at once!

Sapphira: Well, actually, we weren't sure how to do it either! We were just kind of going on instinct. We became kind of like a family—one very big family. There were basically four things Peter asked all the new believers to do: to get sound, biblical teaching from the apostles; to fellowship together (especially with those of us who had been believers longer); to share in the Lord's Supper; and to pray.

Interviewer: Sounds like the exact same things we are encouraged to do even today. How were you able to organize and do all that, given the large number of new converts?

Sapphira: Well, ultimately it really was up to them. We certainly didn't know them all. Nor did we have names and addresses to follow up with them! But we figured that if their salvation had been real, then they would make the effort.

Interviewer: Did they?

Sapphira: Yes—most, if not all of them, did. One of the things we did early on was to make sure there were opportunities for doing so—for getting together, that is. We couldn't just meet together once a week. That would not have been nearly enough. So we tried to have something almost every day. We became sort of a community within a community.

We found ourselves meeting together all the time, every chance we could. Every day we had opportunities for prayer and training. We also met in individual homes to pray and remember Christ through the Lord's Supper, and we shared meals together—lots and lots of meals! Those seemed to be a big hit!

Interviewer: Yes, Christians do like to eat! Even today some of our favorite times together are shared around a potluck dinner. Did you and Ananias have a specific role in any of these opportunities?

Sapphira: Well, as I said, a lot of it wasn't organized. We found ourselves joining in with different groups at different times. Small groups—that was really the best way to get to know people. Ananias and I had been blessed financially, so we had people over for supper nearly every evening. We never once asked them to help pay for the food or to help cook or do the dishes. Mind you, some did, but that wasn't something we asked—we had so much fun giving and sharing and getting to know the newer Christians. And we began to realize that while some of us were well-to-do, a lot of people among us had a hard life. So Ananias and I began selling off extra things we had and sharing with those less fortunate. As you know, that's what eventually got us into trouble.

Interviewer: Please, continue. Tell us what happened.

Sapphira: Well, you have to understand that during this time, Peter and the apostles were performing miracle after miracle. And with each one, the excitement level of all the believers multiplied. Everyone was so excited and happy. We were still growing in numbers by leaps and bounds. And with each growth spurt, we were encouraged to continue to watch out for and care for each other. Ananias and I had already been doing that in smaller ways and had begun to toss around ideas for a way we could help out the church family in a larger way. It was something we both felt led to do, but we weren't quite sure what to do or how to go about doing it. It was because of Barnabas that we got the idea to sell a piece of land.

Interviewer: What did Barnabas do or say to give you that idea? And who was Barnabas anyway?

Sapphira: Well, Barnabas was one of our church leaders. His real name was Joseph. Barnabas was actually the nickname we all gave him because it meant "Son of Encouragement." He truly was an encourager. He always seemed to say or do the right thing, no matter the situation.

As it turned out, Barnabas decided to sell a field he owned and give the proceeds to the church. Believe me, it did encourage the church. To be given so much money at one time was unheard of! That money certainly did go a long way in providing for the less fortunate. And Barnabas got a lot of attention because of it. People were praising him right and left and thanking him for his unselfishness and generosity. But Barnabas seemed so nonchalant about what he had done—almost as if he was unaware of how much he had helped the church. He actually seemed embarrassed at all the attention he was getting.

Now don't misunderstand me, Ananias and I had nothing against Barnabas. We loved him. He truly was a great guy. He was as humble a man as you'll ever find. And his faith was genuine. His decision to sell the field and give the money to the church was made out of pure motives. But as it turned out, his gesture and the response from those in the church— older Christians as well as newer ones—became a huge stumbling block for Ananias and me.

Interviewer: How so? How could something so noble do such harm?

Sapphira: Well, I guess you could say it began as jealousy. Ananias and I had eyes and ears, you know! We saw and heard what Barnabas had done. And we saw and heard all the attention he was getting because of it. We wanted that same attention and recognition for ourselves. After all, we were trying to move up in the church and wanted people to notice us and recognize our efforts just as they had done for Barnabas.

Interviewer: Sounds like the green-eyed monster. Anytime he begins to rear his ugly head, trouble usually isn't far behind.

Sapphira: Oh, you're right about that! Well, Ananias and I sat down to talk one evening, and he said, "You know, we have this huge piece of property on the south side that we're not using. Let's sell it so we'll have a bunch of money to give the church like Barnabas did." So, that's what we set out to do. And it sold pretty quickly, too! After we got the money, we had another talk to determine how much of that to give to the church. It had to be the perfect amount—enough to be noticed and praised, and yet not too much. We wanted to have some money to fall back on in case we needed it.

After much thought and discussion, we finally agreed on what we thought was the perfect figure. It was sure to bring about some "oohs" and "ahhs" from our fellow brothers and sisters—especially if we led them to believe this was all the money we had received from the sale. We wanted them to think, "How marvelous of Ananias and Sapphira to give the church all the money they made from the property sale! How wonderful they are!" And should we be questioned, it was our word against theirs, right?

Interviewer: Wow! That was some scheme! What made you think you could get away with that? And what were you two thinking?

Sapphira: Well, as you know, we didn't get away with it. And as for what we were thinking, we just wanted to look good. We wanted to look better to others than we knew we really were. But our plans fell flat.

Interviewer: So we've heard. Tell us, what happened?

Sapphira: Well, that particular morning, I needed to go to the market to get some fresh food for our meal later that evening. I told Ananias to go ahead to the prayer meeting and teaching time without me and that I would catch up with him later. So Ananias went ahead, taking with him the money we had agreed to give to the church. When the time came to present our gifts and offerings, Ananias went forward and handed Peter the money from the sale of our property. However, Peter did not react as Ananias or I thought he would, given the rather large sum of money we had donated. In our minds, we had envisioned Peter hugging us and thanking us, and the church as a whole erupting into applause.

Instead, Peter began questioning Ananias about it. He had never done that before with any other gifts. Why now? Well, Peter told Ananias that he knew the truth and that what we had done was not a lie just to the church but to God himself! We hadn't looked at it that way before! I guess we had been so blinded by our jealousy of Barnabas and our need to be noticed in the church that that "minor" detail didn't even enter our minds!

Then, about three hours later, after I'd finished my shopping and running back by the house to put things away, I went to meet up with Ananias. But before I could find him, Peter saw me and motioned for me to come to the front. Well, I knew it could only be about one thing—our huge donation. So, I pranced to the front like royalty! Then, as I suspected, Peter asked me about the money and property. I told him exactly the same thing Ananias and I had rehearsed. Yes, we did sell our field, and yes, this was the full amount. As soon as I said that, there was a huge gasp from the church, and the place fell silent. And oh, you should have seen the look on Peter's face! He was so downcast and sorrowful—almost as if he would burst into tears any minute. At the time, I wasn't sure why what we had done was such a horrible thing. After all, we had given a rather large amount. I didn't realize at the time that Peter, and everyone else, knew the whole truth.

Interviewer: What happened next?

Sapphira: Well, Peter just shook his head for what seemed like the longest time, and when he spoke, you could hardly hear him. Oh, I remember it almost word for word. He asked how the two of us could even think of doing such a thing. He pointed out that we had conspired together to test the Spirit of the Lord—the Holy Spirit—the Spirit that had fallen upon everyone just a few short weeks earlier and had brought such rejuvenation and excitement to the church. Then he said, "Just outside that door are the young men who buried your husband. They will carry you out, too."

Interviewer: Oh, my goodness. What did you think then?

Sapphira: Well, I honestly didn't have time to think! I went immediately into shock and died a short time later.

Interviewer: Wow. Sapphira, I don't know what to say. I am so sorry.

Sapphira: Oh, don't be. It's OK. Ananias and I had a good life. It was just cut short because of one very large mistake.

Interviewer: Sapphira, our time is almost up. But before we let you go, we'd like to know what lessons you learned from your life that you could share with us—things that would help us live our lives in better service to God.

Sapphira: Well, a number of things come to mind. First, I'd say beware of what jealousy can make you do. Ananias and I were good Christian people. We loved God, and we loved being with his people and serving in the church. That was our life. But jealousy got the best of us.

That leads me to another very important thought. As Christians, it should never be our goal to seek glory for ourselves. Our number one goal should be to strive to see that God is glorified no matter what we're doing—whether it's giving of our material possessions or our time, or whether it's verbally sharing his glorious nature with others. No matter what, seek God's glory above your own.

Next, beware of misrepresenting yourself. We never did find out exactly how Peter came to know the truth of what we had done. And it really doesn't matter. The truth of the matter is, we lied—not only to our brothers and sisters but also to Peter and the other apostles, and the Holy Spirit. We knew in our hearts that what we were doing wasn't right, but we were so concerned about our reputation that we did all we could do to make sure people saw what we wanted them to see. You know, it wasn't that we held back some of the money that was wrong. After all, it was ours to do with as we wished. And we certainly weren't required to give it to the church. What was wrong and what got us in so much trouble was our claim that it was every penny we had gotten for the land. It was the lie. If we had just given the money and not claimed it to be the entire amount, things would have turned out so differently. But we were consumed with our own praise and glory and recognition.

Lastly, I'd say to keep in mind that you might be able to fool people sometimes, but you can never fool God. God knows your heart. He knows whether your motive in doing something is pure or not.

Interviewer: Sapphira, again, thank you so much for joining us. I'm glad we got to hear your story in your own words. It helps us to see that you were every bit as human as we are today. I'm sure that some of the lessons you learned in your life will help us in our own walk with the Lord.

Sapphira: Oh, you're welcome. And it was my pleasure. And I'm so glad I didn't back out! You have all been such good listeners and understanding in seeing the situation as I lived it.

Interviewer: Thank you, Sapphira.

DISCUSSION QUESTIONS:

1. We learned that part of Ananias and Sapphira's problem was outright jealousy. What exactly is jealousy? In what ways can it become a problem in today's modern church—or have we matured enough to be rid of it?

2. Ananias and Sapphira's initial desire to give more money to the church in the fashion they did was so they would appear "super spiritual" in the eyes of the other Christians in their church and community. Let's suppose they hadn't been caught. Is there really such a thing as getting away with something? Why or why not?

3. Ananias and Sapphira never found out how Peter came to know of their deception. How do you think he found out?

4. While we may like to think we have never done anything even remotely close to what Ananias and Sapphira did, when we look deep into our hearts, I'm sure all of us have disappointed God at one time or another. What are some common ways we disappoint God, whether intentionally or unintentionally?

5. As Christians, we know that the Bible is the inspired Word of God and that everything written in it is there for a reason. Besides jealousy, lying, and the matter of who deserves glory, are there other reasons you can think of for why God may have wanted Luke to include the story of Ananias and Sapphira?

6. Suppose your church had a huge growth spurt of new believers. What are some practical ways Christians of today can go about training, teaching, and incorporating the new believers into their own church family?

Mrs. Manoah (a.k.a. Samson's Mom)

Background Reading: Judges 13:1–16:31
In-Class Reading: Judges 13
Key Verse: Judges 13:7

Interviewer: Welcome, Mrs. Manoah. It is so kind of you to join us. And it is such an honor for us to get to visit with you.

Mrs. Manoah: Why, thank you. Although I must say that I was a bit surprised you wanted to interview me! I had heard through the grapevine that you were interviewing women of the Bible, but I never, ever in my wildest dreams thought that I would be one of them.

Interviewer: And why would that surprise you? After all, you are a woman of the Bible, aren't you?

Mrs. Manoah: Well, yes, I am. I guess I didn't think anyone even remembered I ever existed. It's just that I never considered anything in my life to be of great importance.

Interviewer: Oh, now that's where you're wrong! Of all the hundreds of thousands of women who have ever lived, you are one of a very few who had an angel come and visit her—and you had that experience twice! We can only imagine how amazing that was for you. Will you tell us your story? Why did an angel come to you?

Mrs. Manoah: Well, my husband, Manoah, and I had been married for quite some time, but we had not been able to have children. From the time I was a little girl, that's all I ever wanted—marriage and children. Back in my day, that's about the only thing that made any woman's life of value—her ability to have children and lots of them! My husband and I both wanted a child in the worst way. I had long since given up on having a house full of children. We were getting up in years, and at that point in our lives, I would have been happy to have even one child, boy or girl. I just wanted a baby to hold in my arms.

Then one day, out of the clear blue, this man appeared in front of me and told me I was barren and childless. My first thought was, "How rude! You don't have to rub it in."

I was already feeling pretty down and out of sorts, and I was not having the best of days. Did you ever have one of those days when nothing seemed to be going right? Oh, of course you have. Everyone does! Anyway, to be reminded of this awful fact, by a complete stranger no less, really made my already bad mood even worse. Evidently he could see I had no patience for small talk, because he wasted no time in telling me why he was there. Before I knew it, he had blurted out that I would become pregnant and give birth to a son. I literally froze in my tracks. Eyes wide and mouth hanging open, I just stood there. And what's perhaps even more amazing is that for whatever reason, I believed him! Why, I don't know. Maybe it was his mannerism or the matter-of-fact way in which he said it, but I had absolutely no doubt he knew something I didn't. I believed him instantly! In retrospect, this was quite amazing for me, because I wasn't usually a gullible person—especially with strangers regarding serious issues. And believe me, having a child was a serious issue! Then this man told me the strangest thing—he told me that I needed to go on a strict diet!

Interviewer: A diet! Why, I never heard of such a thing. How insulted you must have felt! Why would he do such a thing? And what kind of a diet did he put you on, anyway?

Mrs. Manoah: Well, he told me that I was not to drink any wine or other fermented drink of any kind or have anything from the grapevine. Nor was I to eat anything unclean.

Interviewer: Did he at least give you a reason as to why you needed to go on this special diet?

Mrs. Manoah: Well, he said it was because of my son— my "son," mind you—who was going to be a very special man. He said my son would be a Nazirite.

Interviewer: Mrs. Manoah, I'm sorry, but I'm still not sure I fully understand. What exactly was a Nazirite, and why would that affect what you ate?

Mrs. Manoah: In a nutshell, a Nazirite was a person who made a vow to be set aside for God's service, and part of that vow involved a list of dietary restrictions. Sometimes a Nazirite vow was temporary—only for a certain period of time. And sometimes people made the vow intending it to be for the rest of their lives. In our case—our son's case—it was literally for life, which is why I was put on this special diet even before I conceived. That way, from the very second of the beginning of my son's life in the womb to his death, he was a Nazirite. There was never a time in his life that he wasn't under the Nazirite vow.

Interviewer: Were there any other stipulations placed upon you or your son?

Mrs. Manoah: Not for me. My son, however, had to carry on with this diet his entire life and was never, ever, to cut his hair.

Interviewer: Why not? To me that seems kind of strange as well.

Mrs. Manoah: Oh, that really wasn't strange at all—at least not for us in my day. It was customary for people who were set aside as Nazirites to not cut their hair during the entire period of their vow. That was another part of the requirements.

Interviewer: OK—let's back up and summarize for a moment. This man shows up, tells you you're going to have a baby, a son, who's destined to be a Nazirite, and puts you on a special diet because of that. What was going through your mind? What did you do then?

Mrs. Manoah: Well, I headed straight for Manoah, of course! I was so excited, I couldn't wait to tell him about the baby—especially since I had been told the baby was going to be a boy. I knew Manoah would be so happy! It wasn't until I started hearing the words come out of my mouth that I realized how absurd my story sounded. And I realized that I had a lot of unanswered questions.

For starters, I didn't know the man's name or where he came from. Then there was the problem of how to describe him. I thought he must have been a man of God, maybe even an angel, but I wasn't sure at the time. After all, I'd never, ever had an angel come to me before—and really never expected to. So, when it came to describing him, I found myself at a loss for words. I finally could only come up with one word to sum up his appearance—"awesome."

Interviewer: Awesome, indeed! What did Manoah do, or think, when you told him what had happened?

Mrs. Manoah: Oh, I wasn't at all sure how Manoah would react. After all, we were living in a time when Israel as a whole wasn't exactly obeying God as it should. And because of that, God had allowed us to become subjected to the Philistines, and evil was becoming more and more prevalent every day. I guess I thought there was a strong chance Manoah wouldn't believe me—after all, God was very unhappy with our nation, so why would he bother with one couple who were struggling to have a baby? How important could that be to God when there was so much else going on?

But Manoah didn't seem to bat an eye. Instead, he took my hands, and we both got on our knees and then Manoah began praying. He didn't doubt or question me at all—not for a second.

Later, when I told my best friend about what had happened, she said Manoah probably could see the difference in me the way she had—that I was already glowing. I don't know if it was from pregnancy or from seeing the angel or both. But you know, I honestly did feel different.

At any rate, Manoah believed me the minute I told him, and he began praying. Unlike a lot of Israel at the time, Manoah was a God-fearing man, and our praying together was not all that unusual. But this time, I thought Manoah was especially bold in his request. I must admit that I wasn't at all sure this particular prayer of his would ever be answered!

Interviewer: My goodness, what did Manoah pray that was so bold and daring?

Mrs. Manoah: Well, he asked for the man of God to be sent back to us so he could tell us how to rear our son. Can you imagine? I mean, really, with his first visit, we'd already been blessed beyond what most people ever experienced. After all, it wasn't every day people had a man of God appear to them. And I don't know that I had ever heard of it happening twice in one day.

Interviewer: And did he? Did the man of God return?

Mrs. Manoah: Oh, yeah, he did—but not as we expected! I guess we both assumed that, if he came back (and that was a big *if*, mind you) it would be to either Manoah or to the two of us together. Instead, he appeared to me while I was out in the field all by myself—again! My first thought was, "Why do you keep popping up when I'm all by myself? Couldn't you at least come when Manoah's around?" But he didn't. Here he was, and here I was, and here Manoah wasn't!

Interviewer: What did you do then?

Mrs. Manoah: Well, I pleaded with the man to stay put and to not go anywhere. I asked him if he would wait while I ran to get Manoah.

Interviewer: Did he agree to wait?

Mrs. Manoah: Yes, he did! However, since I wasn't sure how long he would wait, I ran as fast as I could back to the house to get Manoah. Finally, the two of us got back to the field where I had left the man. And when we did get there, this man was so patient with Manoah. He could tell that Manoah wanted to say something, but Manoah was stumbling over his words. It seemed the harder Manoah tried, the more tongue-tied he became. The man stood there, waiting and smiling.

Interviewer: What was Manoah trying to say?

Mrs. Manoah: Well, by the time we got back to the man, we were both quite out of breath—especially me. After all, in one day I'd already run the length of this field more times than I cared to remember! So, between gasps for air, I introduced Manoah to him. And do you know what Manoah asked him? He turned around and asked the man if he was the one who had talked to me! I couldn't believe it! After all, I had just introduced him as such! Here I was, doubled over, hands on my knees, still trying to catch my breath. When Manoah asked that, I just gave him this sideways glance and thought, "You have got to be kidding! I cannot believe what you just said. You mean to tell me we came running all this way for you to ask him that?" After all, we were in the middle of a field, and he was the only other man around! Hello! Who else did he think this guy could possibly be?

Interviewer: You know, Mrs. Manoah, I can just picture you now. You had to have been appalled! So, what did the man of God say?

Mrs. Manoah: "I am." That's all he said! There was this uncomfortably long pause—you know, the kind where the silence is nearly deafening. Then, finally, Manoah's brain and tongue began to function, and he asked the man what he intended to ask in the first place, which was for more instruction on how we are to bring up our son. Actually, he asked it much more eloquently than that. He said something like, "When your words are fulfilled, what is to be the rule that governs the boy's life and work?" That's not exactly how I would have worded it and that's *not* how Manoah had prayed earlier. But I guess, in this man's presence, Manoah was a bit uncomfortable and felt he needed to sound more dignified than either of us probably looked at the moment!

But you know what struck me about this man of God? He didn't seem to notice our appearance or even what we said or how we said it. Instead, he just talked to us in a manner that was so soothing. His voice was comforting and reassuring. He told

Manoah that I must do all he had already told me to do. In other words—I was still on the diet!

Interviewer: Were you and Manoah disappointed that you didn't get any further details on how to rear your son?

Mrs. Manoah: Maybe a little. But the man of God—an angel, as we were soon to learn—was so reassuring in his voice and the way he acted that somehow, even though he didn't actually say it in words, we knew that we would know what to do when the time came.

Interviewer: What happened next?

Mrs. Manoah: Well, Manoah and I wanted him to let us prepare a goat and feed him. But he wouldn't hear of it. Instead, he told us that if we wanted to, we could offer a burnt offering to the Lord. So that's what we set out to do. Meanwhile, Manoah asked the man what his name was so we would know whom to give the credit to when everything came true.

Interviewer: So, what was his name?

Mrs. Manoah: We still don't know! He wouldn't tell us. Instead, he said that it was "beyond understanding." That was very puzzling, but we didn't pursue it any further. So, we finished gathering supplies for the burnt offering—the goat and some grain—and sacrificed it on a rock to the Lord. Then—oh, you are not going to believe what happened next! It's hard for me to believe even to this day—and I was standing right there watching with my own two eyes! This flame blazed up from the altar and went straight toward heaven! And this man, this angel of the Lord, ascended in the flame. It was at that moment we knew without a doubt that the man had, indeed, been sent by God.

Interviewer: Wow! What happened after that?

Mrs. Manoah: Well, Manoah went straight into panic mode. He began yelling, "We're doomed! We've just seen God! Now we're going to die!"

Interviewer: While Manoah was panicking, what were you thinking? How did you feel?

Mrs. Manoah: Well, I didn't feel that way at all—that we were doomed to die, that is. Actually, I felt just the opposite—that I now had more life than ever before. After all, when you stop to think about it, why would the Lord do all this and tell us all this just to kill us? It just didn't make sense.

Well, as it turned out, I was right. We didn't die (at least not until many, many years later), and I was pregnant. Then several months later, I gave birth to a very precious baby whom we named Samson. And from that moment on, it seems we became known as Samson's mom and dad. I'm sure you've probably heard about him. He's a whole lot more famous than Manoah or I ever was. Anyway, from that point on, our whole lives became wrapped up in the life of that young man.

Interviewer: Oh, of course we know Samson! We've heard about him since our earliest days in Sunday school. Mrs. Manoah, or maybe I should call you

"Samson's mom," our time is almost up. But before we go, as Samson's mother, could you share a quick summary of his life from your perspective?

Mrs. Manoah: Well, Samson struggled a lot. And it hurt like crazy to see him make his mistakes. Manoah and I had done the best we knew how in rearing him. But it was still so hard to sit back and watch him struggle. Keep in mind that Israel was still going through a rebellious time of spiritual and moral decay. And there were very few godly examples for Samson to follow. Manoah and I had tried to live as we should, and we did our best to instill in him the importance of not only following the outward appearances in fulfilling the Nazirite vow but also striving for inner holiness. We wanted him to understand the importance of surrendering his will to God. That's one area he struggled so much with—his will vs. God's will.

But in the end, God was able to accomplish his will through Samson, in spite of his weaknesses or any parenting mistakes Manoah or I made along the way. And just before his death, Samson reconnected with God and decided to be obedient. Samson finally prayed for God's strength, and then the two of them together managed to kill more Philistines in one moment than Samson had throughout his entire lifetime. Samson's life was proof that it's never too late to surrender and be obedient to God.

Interviewer: Mrs. Manoah, how rewarding it must be for you to know your son had been used of God in such a mighty way. It has been such a joy visiting with you and hearing your remarkable story. Before we let you go, do you have some words of wisdom you could share with today's woman—anything that might encourage us or help us in our Christian walk?

Mrs. Manoah: Well, I would first stress obedience to God. Do what God is telling you to do, whether you understand it at the moment or not. And if you're not sure what you're supposed to do—ask him! Then stop and listen to him. He'll tell you! And if you're playing the "battle of the wills" game with God, give up, surrender, and go ahead and let him win—he's going to anyway, you know. So save yourself some frustration and heartache and do what he wants you to do.

Then I would say, if there are any mothers out there beating themselves up because of their wayward child, stop. If you did the best you knew to do in bringing up your child, turn him or her over to God. You are not responsible for their poor choices, just as your parents are not responsible for any of your own choices. Trust God. He loves your child as much as you do—more, actually! He has a plan for the life of that child of yours, and he can work his plan in spite of any side roads your child wanders along. Even through their mistakes—or yours—God is able to work. Just continue to set a good example and pray, pray, pray. God can turn their life around regardless of how dismal it may look now.

Interviewer: Mrs. Manoah, thank you so much for joining us. Visiting with you has been a joy, and we have learned so much from you. Thank you for your insights and for your willingness to share with us.

DISCUSSION QUESTIONS:

1. Mrs. Manoah seemed shocked that God would take the time or make the effort to bother with her and her problems and concerns. Can you think of a time when God surprised you by answering a prayer that at the time seemed so trivial you were almost ashamed to ask God about it?

2. When Mrs. Manoah told her husband about the man's visit and what he had told her, he immediately believed her. Why do you think that was?

3. Even though he shared no new information, the angel came back to Mrs. Manoah a second time. Why do you think he did that? And why do you think he chose to show up again when Mrs. Manoah was alone, even though he apparently was willing to talk to Manoah as well?

4. In the presence of the angel, Manoah found himself speaking more formally than normal. Why do you think people tend to sound "fancier" when they're praying in public? Is it wrong?

5. How can you be certain you know what God's will is for you?

6. Let's pretend there is a board game called "Battle of the Wills." The starting point is a place called "Your Will" and the finish line is a place called "God's Will." There are 50 stepping stones between. Think about which stone you would say you're on. What experiences have you gone through in your life that have helped to move you along the path to 100 percent

surrender and full obedience to God's will for your life?

Mrs. Lot

Background Reading: Genesis 11:27–19:38
In-Class Reading: Genesis 13:5-13; 18:20-19:29
Key Verse: Genesis 19:26

Interviewer: Welcome, Mrs. Lot. We are so glad you are able to be with us today. The past few weeks we have been talking to Bible women and hearing their story in their own words. All we've really ever known about you has been what little bit Moses recorded. Would you mind filling in a few of the blanks? We are especially curious about your early years with Lot.

Mrs. Lot: Thank you for inviting me. Let me see . . . where do I begin? Well, when we were first married, Lot and I did a lot of traveling. That was something I really came to hate. All the packing and moving got to be overwhelming. At first, when we were young, it was romantic. We were always going to new lands and meeting new people. But after a while, all the living out of a suitcase, so to speak, really got to be old.

Interviewer: Why were you always on the move?

Mrs. Lot: It's a long story, but I'll try to give you a quick version. Lot had had a rough childhood. His mother had died giving birth to him, and his father, Haran, died not too many years later. So Lot went to live with his grandfather, Terah. Well, Terah decided to move his family from Ur of the Chaldeans (where Lot grew up) to Canaan. But before they could get there, they had to stop because Terah became sick. Then he died. This left Lot orphaned yet again. But Abram and Sarai, Lot's uncle and aunt, took him in. It was shortly after this—maybe two or three years—that I met and married Lot, and we began to accumulate our own possessions—servants, sheep, livestock—you know, your normal stuff.

Then, Uncle Abram decided to go ahead and move his family on to Canaan to fulfill the dream his father had had. And because we were young and newly married, the thought of travel intrigued us, so we tagged along.

Interviewer: Did Abram or Sarai encourage you to stay put—to stay where you were and start your own family?

Mrs. Lot: Oh, we could have stayed. But we were so young and adventurous that travel seemed so much more romantic. Actually, there never really was much of a discussion. Besides, Uncle Abram and Aunt Sarai didn't have any children of their own, so they had kind of adopted Lot and me as their children. That was another reason to move—to stay close to Uncle Abram and Aunt Sarai. So we all traveled to Canaan and settled in a town called Bethel. That's where our two daughters were born.

Anyway, we hadn't been there very long when the entire country suffered a famine. So we all packed up and headed to Egypt, planning to stay only until the famine was over.

Interviewer: How long did that turn out to be?

Mrs. Lot: Not nearly long enough! That move was especially hard on me, because now I had to keep track of two curious toddlers. Anyway, we no sooner got to Egypt's borders than Uncle Abram and Egypt's Pharaoh had a "difference of opinion," so to speak, and we were promptly escorted out of the country—by armed guards, nonetheless! I had never been so embarrassed in my life. It seemed everyone was looking and pointing at us as we scampered about packing up our things and loading the donkeys!

Finally we were far enough away that the armed escorts left us, and not knowing where else to go, we headed back to Bethel, even though we knew life would still be hard. After all, the land was only beginning to recover from its serious drought. The traveling was so hard on the girls. And Uncle Abram and Aunt Sarai weren't getting any younger, you know! All the traveling was taking a toll on everyone. Tempers began to get a little testy, and our patience was beginning to wear thin. But we finally made it back to Bethel. And I began unpacking—again!

Interviewer: Sounds to me like you did an awful lot of unnecessary traveling—especially if you ended up back at the exact same place where you started and still had to endure the effects of a famine!

Mrs. Lot: Maybe yes. Maybe no. We don't know what would have happened had we stayed. The famine had been pretty severe. Some think Uncle Abram jumped the gun and ran off to Egypt, not trusting the Lord to take care of us. I don't know. When does one ever really know for sure? Bottom line—we all do what we think is best at the time we are faced with any uncertain situation.

Anyway, we—Lot and I—trusted Uncle Abram. He was always trying to do what God wanted and was always listening for the Lord's voice to guide him. To finally get back home was all I really cared about. I had never been so happy to get unpacked and settled in my life!

Interviewer: I can imagine that had to be frustrating for you—all that traveling around in circles!

Mrs. Lot: Oh, it was. But as it turned out, we all became masters in patience, and we did prosper financially along the way as well. So, it wasn't all a waste! Both Uncle Abram and Lot became very wealthy during the months we were gone, with more sheep, cattle, servants, silver, gold—lots of things. But you know, it was actually because of that wealth that we ended up moving yet again!

Interviewer: Oh no! And just when I thought we had you all settled for good! What now? How did your wealth cause you to have to move on?

Mrs. Lot: Well, remember, the land had just gone through severe famine. And while the water and crops were beginning to get back to normal, they still had a ways to go. Finding enough water and grain to feed all the livestock became a full-time, frustrating job for the herdsmen. To stop all the arguing and fighting among them, Uncle Abram suggested we split up and go our separate ways.

Interviewer: That sounds like a reasonable plan. How did you go about deciding to make the split?

Mrs. Lot: One day Uncle Abram asked Lot to go for a walk with him. They were walking along, making small talk, when Uncle Abram suddenly stopped! Lot asked him what was wrong—if he was feeling all right. Uncle Abram assured him he was OK and then began talking about the situation—the overcrowding. Lot agreed. He knew something needed to be done, but he didn't know what—and being the younger of the two, he certainly didn't feel like it was his place to suggest a different arrangement.

Anyway, Uncle Abram told Lot what he thought the only solution was. He pointed out the fact that the land to the East, the Jordan Valley, was fertile and well watered, and suggested that one of them go there while the other remained in Canaan.

Interviewer: And what did Lot think of that?

Mrs. Lot: Oh, at first Lot wasn't too keen on that idea at all! He just knew Uncle Abram would want to go where the land was better and life would be easier. And being the senior member of the family, it certainly was his right to choose the best spot. But that's not what he suggested at all. Instead, he looked Lot square in the eyes and told him to choose. At first, I think Lot thought it was a trick. On the one hand, you would have plenty of water and food for your family, livestock, and servants. On the other hand, life would be a struggle. But Lot knew his Uncle Abram loved him and wanted him to be happy. It took Lot all of about two seconds to say, "I'll take the Jordan Valley."

Interviewer: Which, of course, meant yet another move. How did Lot break that news to you? You had to have been getting so tired of this!

Mrs. Lot: Oh, believe me, I was! The traveling that once was so glamorous and romantic was now anything but. It was now a chore! Then Lot pointed out all the advantages. When he mentioned living in a big city, that cinched it for me. Finally, this girl could do some major shopping!

Interviewer: Surely that's not all you thought about!

Mrs. Lot: Oh, of course not—there were also the parties! We could now get a more permanent home than the tent we had been lugging around, and I wouldn't have to be ashamed to have people over anymore. Just think . . . an actual house, with doors and windows and everything! It was like a dream come true!

Interviewer: Wow! I hadn't thought of that. How soon did you get to move?

Mrs. Lot: Well, not soon enough! I was so excited. I began packing immediately. And I packed endlessly until we were all ready. It seemed my energy level skyrocketed almost overnight. There was no holding me down. I couldn't wait to get settled into our new home and get on with the life I'd always dreamed.

Interviewer: You know, I can't help but think about what Sarai must have been feeling. Surely she was disappointed. After all, she had been living in tents a whole lot longer than you had.

Mrs. Lot: Yes, I think she was a bit disappointed. But she was also happy at the same time. Both she and Uncle Abram loved Lot like the son they never had. Actually, they did have a son many years later, but that's another story—and one you'd be wise to ask Aunt Sarai about. She was quite a character! Anyway, Uncle Abram and Aunt Sarai wanted more than anything for Lot to be happy and successful. I'm sure she understood my excitement. However, when I was around her, I did try to tone things down a bit, but it was so hard!

Interviewer: You do seem to be a rather bubbly person. I'll bet reining in your excitement was one of the hardest things you had to do!

So, you get moved and settled. Then what? Was life as you thought it would be?

Mrs. Lot: Oh, my goodness, yes! I loved it! When it was all said and done, I was a bit apprehensive the day we finally did make the move. What if we didn't fit in? After all, we had been country folks for a long time. What if they didn't like us? What if the girls couldn't find playmates? What if I couldn't find a best friend to talk with? There were a hundred questions that popped up in my head at the last minute. But you know, it didn't take long at all for us to fit right in. Granted, our wealth probably didn't hurt any. People always seem to be drawn to money. Deep down, I knew that some of my "friends" were only hanging out with me because of my status as a wealthy woman. But you know, I really didn't care. I was more interested in the prestige I had—a nice big house, a handsome husband, two beautiful daughters, and lots of friends. I wanted to be everybody's friend. I wanted everyone to like me. And I did everything I could to see that they did.

Interviewer: Like what kind of things? What did you do to make yourself stand out?

Mrs. Lot: Well, besides making sure we had one of the largest homes around, I flaunted money in other ways, too. I entertained a lot. And I made sure the girls and I always had the latest colorful fashions and tons of jewelry. And Lot, well, I made sure he was always dressed in his finest and that he mingled as much as he could with the other men of Sodom—especially the important men.

Interviewer: Mrs. Lot, it sounds to me like your life took a 180-degree turn from what it had been just a few years before. Were you truly happy—or was it all pretend and show?

Mrs. Lot: I admit that at first I was a bit uncomfortable. After all, if people found out, what would they think of our previous near nomadic lifestyle? If instead of adoring me and envying me, they pitied me? It was hard early on. In order to blend in, we kept secret so many things from our past. But as time passed, the memories passed as well. It got easier—too easy, in fact.

Interviewer: What do you mean?

Mrs. Lot: Well, we began to live the lie. It was almost as if the Lot and Mrs. Lot we used to be no longer existed, and we were now the new and improved, rich man Lot and his wife who lived in the wealthiest suburb of Sodom. We had become so entangled in this lifestyle that the new "us" no longer prayed or worshipped the Lord. In fact, the new "us" hardly gave the Lord a thought at all until—.

Interviewer: Until what? What happened?

Mrs. Lot: Well, one evening several years after we had moved to Sodom, Lot met a couple of men at the city gate and invited them home. Lot and I had become well-known for our hospitality, so it wasn't unusual for Lot to bring people home for supper. Shortly after we had finished eating, we began to hear quite a commotion at the front door. When Lot went to find out what was going on, he was appalled! Some men in town were demanding that Lot turn the two men over to them. Well, we knew they were up to no good, so Lot refused. But they insisted. Finally they lunged at Lot and tried to break down the door. Then, the two men—angels, as we later learned—reached out and pulled Lot back inside and bolted the door. They caused the men outside to become blind so they couldn't break in.

The girls and I were terrified! Then the angels told us why they were there—that the city had become so sinful and corrupt and so detestable to the Lord that he was going to destroy it.

Interviewer: What did you think or feel when they told you this?

Mrs. Lot: At first, I couldn't think clearly at all! I was so terrified. Then I began to have this sadness come over me. After all, we had become friends with so many people in this town. My best friend lived just down the street, our daughters were engaged to be married, and the house was just as I wanted it to be. Life was going so well. But deep down, Lot and I knew things weren't right. We knew we had strayed from the Lord. But we liked our new, comfortable lifestyle. Even though we knew we were wrong, we liked it. We enjoyed it. However, I don't think we realized just how numb we had become to sin. Does that make any sense?

Interviewer: More than you realize. There's a lot of ways I think we can identify with you and what you were going through. One of the big issues of today is the question of what constitutes a family. Some people argue that it's not just a man and a woman, but two men or two women could establish a family. Some Christians today have become so tolerant that they seem to have lost sight of the "love the sinner, but hate the sin" concept. Maybe they haven't gotten to the point that they "love" the sin, but many have become tolerant and accepting of it.

Mrs. Lot: Then you do know what I mean! It's hard—especially when that is all that's around you. Up until the angels pointed that out, we hadn't realized that we were the only ones who still had an ounce of morality left. We had been told that the Lord would save the city if only 10 innocent people could be found. Do you know how many God found? Four! In the big city of Sodom, only four—Lot, me, and our two daughters. That's all! Not even our future sons-in-law believed. And you know, I'm not so sure how "innocent" we were. We certainly had strayed from what we knew was right. But the Lord was gracious and merciful to us. That was made very clear to us the next morning.

Interviewer: How? What happened then?

Mrs. Lot: Well, after things finally settled down that evening, the men told us to get some rest because the next day we would need to leave before the city was destroyed. Yeah, right! Who could rest with all this about to happen? I think I must have been in a state of shock because I couldn't seem to do anything except walk through the house and look at everything. We had been told not to take anything with us except the clothes on our backs. So, I didn't need to pack. Instead, I spent the night pacing the floor, crying, feeling sorry for myself, and fingering our possessions one last time.

The girls were so concerned about their fiancés that finally Lot went out to try to convince them to leave with us as well. But they wouldn't. Actually, they didn't even believe him—they thought he was joking. Little did they know that Lot had never been more serious about anything in his life! So Lot finally gave up, came back home, and broke the news to the girls.

Interviewer: How were the girls handling the suddenness of all of this—especially given this latest news about their fiancés?

Mrs. Lot: Oh, they were devastated. Being young and impressionable, they had become acclimated to the lifestyle even more than Lot or I had. And to now lose their dreams of marriage and children only compounded their loss.

Interviewer: I can only imagine. It had to have been so hard for you to leave. How were you ever able to do it—especially since you didn't know where you were headed?

Mrs. Lot: Actually, we found it impossible to leave—all of us. If it hadn't been for the angels, I'm sure we would have all been killed when the city was destroyed.

Interviewer: What did the angels do?

Mrs. Lot: Well, at dawn, the angels began yelling at us—telling us to hurry up and get out—to leave the city immediately! But we couldn't seem to move—not one of us! Our feet seemed glued to the floor. Finally, the angels took us by the hands and literally forced us out of the city. All the while they were telling us to run for our lives—to run and not look back. The Lord was so merciful to reach out and save us as he did. Finally, it was as if everything clicked—our brains, our feet—everything! And we began to run as hard and as fast as we could. That's when it happened.

Interviewer: That's when what happened?

Mrs. Lot: That's when the sky began to turn brilliant shades of red, yellow, and orange, and we began to hear all kinds of sounds like buildings crumbling and people screaming. It was so horrible. Now Lot was the one who was yelling, "Run, run! Don't look back.

Just keep running. Faster, faster!" I heard him, and I wanted to keep running. And I tried not to look back. Honestly, I did. But I couldn't resist.

Interviewer: Why? Lot and the angels all told you not to. What were you thinking?

Mrs. Lot: I don't know. Did you ever have one of those moments when you knew you shouldn't do something and everything in and around you was telling you not to? But you did it anyway? That's what was going on. I just wanted to see my home one last time. I guess I was scared of what the future would hold. I didn't know where we were headed or what we were going to do. How could we start all over with only the clothes on our backs? I just couldn't seem to let go of the past. I guess I just thought one little glance wouldn't hurt. I didn't plan to stare—or even to look. It was just a peek. One quick, short, little peek. But that's all it took. My life ended with that one little, seemingly harmless glance.

Interviewer: Wow. And you know, it's that little peek that left you immortalized forever in history. In fact, I'm sure that before our interview started, all most of us could tell about you or your life was that you were the woman who was turned into a pillar of salt.

Mrs. Lot, we have certainly enjoyed visiting with you and getting to know you. Scripture only gives us the hard facts about you and your life. You have allowed us to see the personality behind the woman we've only known as "Lot's wife." Before we let you go, could you summarize a few lessons from your life that we modern-day women would do well to remember?

Mrs. Lot: My goodness—where do I begin? There are so many! Hmmm. I guess one would be that, as Christians, never let wealth lure you away from God. Lot and I were not spiritually mature enough to handle either our wealth or a city such as Sodom— not many people are.

I would also tell you to beware of drowning out God's voice with other things. I realize now that that's exactly what I had been doing under the disguise of "entertaining." As long as I had people around or filled my days with "busyness," I didn't have to hear—or listen to—the still, small voice inside of me. I would urge you to listen to God. Whatever he tells you to do—do it. Be obedient. If he tells you to move, move! If he tells you not to look, don't! I was disobedient and paid for it with my life. Don't you go and do the same. Learn from my mistakes.

Then, lastly, I would say to let go of the past. If God is leading you in a new direction, don't let your fear of the future stop you as it did me. Keep your eyes focused on God and the direction he is leading you in. Once you do that, you can be confident that everything will work out.

Interviewer: Thank you so much, Mrs. Lot. Thank you for sharing so openly and honestly about your life. You have truly been a blessing to us.

DISCUSSION QUESTIONS:

1. Lot's wife was turned into a pillar of salt during a deliberately disobedient moment. Fortunately for us today, God doesn't turn us into a pillar of salt when we deliberately disobey him. However, if he did, what would some of our "statues" catch us looking like?

2. Lot and his wife seemed to justify their tolerance of sin as a small price to pay in order to live the affluent lifestyle they desired. Besides the question of what constitutes a family, what are some other issues in which Christians today are being slowly desensitized?

3. Mrs. Lot gave in to the urge to take one last peek at Sodom. Why do you think she found this command to not look back so hard? If God were to ask you to move on to something else in your life, how hard would it be to let go of the past? Can you hold on to pieces of your old life as you move forward with God? Why or why not?

4. Very often we hear people ask God for a direct sign to confirm what he wants them to do. Mrs. Lot got that. She literally had an angel's hand pulling her away from Sodom and leading her to her future. Even with that, she looked back. Have you ever received a clear, direct sign from God about something? If so, what was it, and how hesitant were you still to follow through?

5. Too often we see only the positive side of things and not the negative. If you had the chance to change your life overnight and become a millionaire, would you?

Why or why not? How much of a factor is age? Do you think the older a person is the better they are able to handle wealth—sudden or not? Why or why not?

6. Mrs. Lot insinuated that even though their trip to Egypt seemed like a waste of time and energy to us, maybe there was a purpose for it that they weren't aware of at the time. Have you ever had something similar happen to you—for which you didn't (or maybe still don't) fully understand the reason?

Mary and Martha

Background Reading: Luke 10:38-42 and John
11:1-45
In-Class Reading: Luke 10:38-42 and John
11:1-7; 17-45
Key Verses: Luke 10:41-42

Interviewer: Ladies, we are so glad that the two of you were willing and able to join us this morning. Our interviews so far have been with just one woman at a time, so it is especially exciting to have two sisters joining us! Tell us, how did the two of you come to know Jesus so well?

Martha: Actually, it was because of our brother, Lazarus.

Mary: You see, one day Lazarus heard Jesus speaking and was so excited about what he was teaching that he invited Jesus home to learn more. I think he also wanted to introduce Martha and me to Jesus so we could get to know him, too.

Martha: I'll never forget that day! I was so embarrassed! We were totally unprepared for company. I had no bread baking, and the house was a complete disaster! I was utterly humiliated!

Mary: Now, Martha, you know Jesus didn't care one bit about that! And besides, your definition of a complete disaster is a far cry from what it actually was. One speck of dust or one sandal out of place does not a disaster make!

Martha: I know. I know. But it still bothers me. We were three grown adults. You would think we could have taken better care of the place!

Interviewer: Ladies, I hate to interrupt, but could you tell me your first impression of Jesus? What did you think of him when you first met and heard him speak? Were you as enthralled with him as Lazarus apparently was?

Mary: Oh my, yes! I could see exactly why Lazarus insisted that Jesus come home with him. To hear Jesus teach was absolutely wonderful. It was spell-binding.

Martha: Yes, it was wonderful. But the surprise of his visit had put me in a bit of a frenzy, and try as I might, I could only give Jesus half-hearted attention. My mind kept thinking about the bread not baking and what I could offer Jesus to eat instead. And my eyes kept going to the sandals in the middle of the floor and the robe tossed into the corner instead of hanging on the hook. Oh, how I wished they would just disappear! How I wished I had picked them up sooner. But they weren't mine, and I had been waiting for Mary or Lazarus to do it. After all, it was their mess!

Honestly, some days those two could really infu-
riate me. I got so tired of picking up after them. But
then, for Lazarus to choose that time to bring home a
guest—I was nearly beside myself!

Interviewer: Martha, I hate to interrupt, but I understand that after that first encounter, Lazarus and Jesus
became very good friends and that Jesus came to your
house quite often. Did it get any easier for you?

Martha: Oh, please don't misunderstand me. I really
did love entertaining. And I really did love to have
Jesus and his disciples come over. Sometimes we
knew Jesus was coming. That, I liked. Other times,
however, Jesus just dropped by unannounced at what
seemed to be the worst possible time. That I didn't
like so much.

Interviewer: Like the time we just read about?

Martha: Yes, that was awful. It had been a while since
Jesus had stopped by, so it wasn't that we were
surprised to see him. It's just that I so desperately
wanted to feed him and his disciples the best meal
ever. Jesus had been to our house often enough that
I'd learned what some of his favorite foods were. So
I made it my goal that day to make a big dinner for
him with some of his favorite dishes, thinking that
would really please him. After all, he didn't get a lot
of home-cooked meals!

Anyway, I was getting stressed out about the
meal. I wanted so badly for everything to be perfect.
And absolutely nothing seemed to be going right.
I began getting more frustrated by the minute. And
Mary—where was Mary? In the living room with the

men. Once again, the sole responsibility of doing the kitchen work had fallen to me. I was making as much racket as I could, trying to give Mary the hint that I needed her help. That didn't work. So I finally just went right in and asked Mary to help me. Which she did—kind of! She'd come in for about 30 seconds, did what I specifically asked her to do, and then, before I knew it, she had wandered back to Jesus. She knew what had to be done, but she wasn't stepping up and doing her share of the work. In fact, she was hardly any help at all!

Interviewer: Mary, is this true? Surely Martha's exaggerating somewhat.

Mary: Well, it's mostly true. But in my defense, it was so hard not to be in the same room as Jesus. When he was around, he lit up the room. And he was like this magnet I was being drawn to. He was always so interesting when he talked—and funny! He had this dry sense of humor that would catch you off guard, and before you knew it, you'd be laughing so hard tears would run down your cheeks. I didn't want to miss any of it.

Martha: And you think I did? I would have liked listening to Jesus, too. But there were responsibilities—and someone had to take care of them. The bread wasn't going to bake itself, you know! I guess I just expected more from you. After all, Mom had taught us that a woman's place was in the kitchen.

Mary: Now, Martha, you knew that kitchen work was not something I specialized in—that was always your area. You've known since we were kids that I would much rather be working outside in the gardens and flower beds or socializing instead of being confined to a tiny little kitchen. And besides, who wants to spend all their time baking? There seemed to be more important things to do than bake bread all the time.

Martha: Yes, I know. But still, under special circumstances—like when Jesus came to visit—it seems you could have "suffered" a little and offered more help.

Interviewer: I can see now, with the two of you, it's going to be hard to get a word in edgewise. It sounds as if we've hit a tender spot with both of you. Martha, you were explaining your frustrations. Please, go on.

Martha: Well, finally it got to the point where I couldn't take it any longer. I was so mad I thought I would explode! I had tried to get Mary away from Jesus to help me and found that didn't work—it was only short-term, minimal help. So I figured the only other thing I could do was to go to Jesus directly. Jesus would know how important it was for us to be serving him. And I knew Mary would do whatever Jesus told her to do. So, I boldly marched right into the living room and asked Jesus if he didn't think that it was unfair for me to be doing all the work while Mary just sat around doing nothing.

Interviewer: You didn't! Martha, what in the world were you thinking?

Mary: Oh, she did all right! I was stunned—and embarrassed. Perhaps I should have been helping more, but I couldn't seem to help myself. I kept being drawn back to Jesus. Then, when Martha came in and "tattled" on me, I was so ashamed of myself.

Martha: I did not tattle! I was merely pointing out that if we were to eat anything decent anytime soon, I needed to have you helping me in the kitchen. That wasn't too much to ask. I was merely expressing my thoughts to Jesus. Hadn't he been telling us that we could do just that—express our deepest thoughts and desires to him? Didn't he want us to be totally open and honest with him?

Mary: Well, yes, but I'm not sure that's what he meant. At any rate, I was embarrassed to no end. So I started to get up and go help. But then Jesus told me to stay put—to stay right where I was. Then he basically told Martha to get over it.

Martha: He did not!

Mary: Well, maybe not in those exact words, but what he said meant pretty much the same thing.

Interviewer: Martha, what did he say to you?

Martha: Well, he basically pointed out that I was allowing myself to get too upset over the details when there was something much more important that I was missing out on entirely.

Interviewer: Which was?

Martha: Jesus himself. He showed me how my priorities were a bit skewed. All along I had been more concerned and spent more time doing things for Jesus than taking the time being with him. I was basically a "doer" and not a "be-er." Jesus said there was a time to "do" and a time to "be" and that this was a "be" moment.

Interviewer: What did you do then?

Martha: Well, I swallowed my pride and did the right thing. I plopped right down on the nearest cushion and began listening to Jesus. I finally began to learn to *be* with Jesus.

Interviewer: What happened to your big, fancy meal?

Martha: Oh, it waited until Jesus was done teaching. Then I served what I had. It was no longer fancy. Nor was it as much as I'd planned, but it was more than enough.

Mary: Actually, I thought it turned out to be one of the best meals you ever cooked!

Martha: That's only because we were all so hungry! By the time we ate, anything would have tasted good— even stale bread!

Mary: Well, whatever the reason, it was good, and Jesus did keep coming back for more.

Martha: He did seem to enjoy it, didn't he? That was really all I wanted in the first place—to please him. I just hadn't learned where to draw the line between the doing and the being.

Mary: I think we both learned a lesson that day! While I was busy being with Jesus that particular time, I realized that, at other times, it probably would be more appropriate or beneficial for me to be doing things for him instead. I guess we discovered that it is important for women to be well-rounded and a balance of both of our personalities in order to best serve God. Learning to be more of a doer was not easy for me. I had to learn to anticipate the needs of others and see where my hands could be put to good use. I had always been one who didn't do a lot of preparation for company. Instead I just kind of winged it. I learned that I needed to think more about people's needs—and to anticipate how I could help meet those needs.

Martha: And learning to take the time to be with Jesus when I should or as often as I should was not an easy thing for me at the time. I had to fight the urge to say yes to every request. I was such the perfectionist and control freak that I very often took over and did things myself just because I knew I could do it and do it right. I learned that others needed the opportunity to serve as well. And as long as I was taking over, they felt too intimidated to serve. I also found I needed to slow down so I could have more time with Jesus. It was not an easy thing for me to do, either. At first I felt really uneasy. I felt guilty anytime I was sitting still. But I did consciously make the effort to sit back and allow myself to refuel, and it sure paid off later.

Interviewer: How so?

Martha: Well, like the time when Lazarus became so sick. That was really a tough time for us. We weren't sure what would happen to us if he died. After all, he was the man of the house. How were two single women going to make it without a man around?

Mary: Oh, those were some very scary days, all right. Both of us were waiting on him hand and foot, doing all we knew to make him better. But nothing we did seemed to work. He seemed to be getting worse. Finally, we decided that the only thing we could do was to send word to Jesus, letting him know how seriously ill Lazarus had become. We just knew that he could heal him. And we thought he would come the minute he found out how sick Lazarus actually was.

Martha: But one day passed and then another. Meanwhile Lazarus was getting sicker and sicker. In the end, he became so sick that he died.

Mary: We were devastated. We were confused. We had so many questions. Why had Lazarus gotten sick? Why couldn't we help him? Why didn't Jesus come? What could we have done differently? We couldn't answer any of them.

Martha: Meanwhile, we had so many people come to the house to mourn with us. It was amazing. We knew Lazarus was loved and respected by many people, but we hadn't realized just how many. Burying Lazarus — putting him in that tomb — was the hardest thing we had ever done. Our hearts ached so much for him. And our minds — well, we were just going through the motions. We couldn't have put two clear thoughts together, even if we'd tried! We were so thankful for our friends who supported and comforted us during that time.

Interviewer: Yes, I agree. Having the comfort and the strength of Christian friends is invaluable during times of heartache or hardship. It's one of the blessings we Christians have, and it makes us wonder how non-Christians ever survive tragedy without it. There's nothing quite like having the support of Christian friends.

Martha: That's so true. But there is something even better—that's having Jesus to lean on. And that's what we were able to do, emotionally and physically. Four days after we had buried Lazarus, I learned that Jesus was on his way to see us. My first instinct was to run down the road to meet him, which is exactly what I did. I didn't even think to tell Mary or—get this!—to tidy up the kitchen! My, how things had changed!

Anyway, when I finally got to Jesus, all I could do was ask him why he hadn't come sooner and say that he could have healed Lazarus. Instead of answering me directly, he told me that Lazarus would rise again. At the time, my mind was so confused that I couldn't understand what he was telling me. Then Jesus reminded me who he was and asked if I believed. Of course I did. Then he asked me to go and get Mary.

Mary: All this time I had been in the house with some of the other mourners. I had no clue what was going on until Martha came back and whispered that Jesus wanted to see me. I was so excited that he had finally come. So I rushed out and ran to meet him, just as Martha had done.

Martha: But this time, we had quite a following! This time, all the mourners were running behind us. They apparently thought we were headed to the tomb. When Jesus saw our entourage coming, all weeping and wailing, He began crying as well. He asked us to take him to the tomb. Once we got there, he asked the men to roll away the stone from the entrance. I couldn't keep quiet any longer. I had to speak up! I reminded Jesus how long Lazarus had been dead and that by now he would smell awful. But that didn't faze Jesus one bit.

Mary: Not one bit. Can you believe it? He wasn't at all concerned about the smell. Instead, he began praying to God and then shouted, "Lazarus, come out!" His booming command nearly scared me to death!

Martha: And Lazarus walked right out of that tomb! He was still wrapped from head to toe, but we could tell it was him. We both nearly fainted! Believe me, the minute he was unwrapped and we saw his face, we both ran straight for him. We couldn't hug him tight enough.

Mary: We were really quite a sight. Here Lazarus was, trying to make his way to Jesus, with two teary-eyed women hanging all over him! But Jesus understood. When we looked into his eyes, there was that twinkle again. And his smile told us that everything would always be all right—no matter what happened.

Interviewer: Ladies, you have no idea how much I hate this, but our time is almost up, and we're going to have to bring this interview to a close. You both seem so passionate about Jesus. Could you summarize a lesson or two from your lives that modern-day women could apply to their own lives? What lesson did you learn that we would be wise to learn?

Mary: I would say the biggest lesson I learned was to strike a balance between doing and being. I had to learn to volunteer and help out more. I realized that while it's important to be with Jesus—or people in general—and to listen to them, it's also important to anticipate their needs and try to meet them. That wasn't easy for me. I felt awkward at first—and very unsure of myself. I was always afraid I wasn't doing or saying the right things. But in the end, I found out that wasn't a valid fear. I learned I could do lots of things. And the more I did, the more confident I became. In the end, I was a much happier person.

Martha: And I learned to back off from some of the physical duties and allow myself more time to be alone with Jesus—to fellowship and communicate with him. And not just with him, but to be that way with other people as well. While doing things for others is good—and appreciated—sometimes all people really want is to have someone take the time and listen to them. I had filled my days with so much work that there wasn't room for Jesus! I also had to realize that I wasn't the only person who could do the work, whatever it was. I finally admitted to myself that my way was not the only way! I learned to step back so others could step forward.

Interviewer: Mary, Martha—thank you so much for joining us. You have both been such a tremendous blessing. Thank you for sharing openly with us and allowing us the opportunity to get to know the two of you better. It's been such a pleasure.

DISCUSSION QUESTIONS:

1. Balance. Both Mary and Martha express the impor-tance of learning to balance their lives between doing for Jesus and being with Jesus. Which one do you think had the hardest time learning her lesson? Is it harder for a "be-er" to learn to step up and be more of a "doer," or vice-versa?

2. The "Marys" in a church may argue that it is hard for her to learn to anticipate needs, and she feels uncom-fortable volunteering and taking on new tasks. She's not sure of herself or not sure that she is capable. How could her transition into becoming more of a doer be made easier by the "Marthas" in church?

3. The "Marthas" may argue that it is just as hard for them to step back and trust others to do the task—it's easier for them to do the job themselves. That way they know it's getting done and getting done right. How could their transition into becoming more of a "be-er" be made easier by the "Marys" in church?

4. Martha justified her "tattling" on Mary by saying that Jesus wants us to be comfortable enough with him to express our deepest thoughts and desires. Do you think Martha was right to do this in front of all the disciples in the room? Is there a right time or place to honestly express ourselves to Jesus? How hard is it for you to be the real "you" when talking with him?

5. At the tomb, we find Martha, always the one for detail, once again speaking her mind when she told Jesus that Lazarus would smell terrible by then. Judging by

what she said, what main point—or points—was she still missing?

6. What is your makeup—are you a Martha, working on developing your Mary traits, or are you a Mary trying to become more like Martha? Do you think having a balance of both traits means you have to have an equal amount of both? Why or why not?

Hannah

Background Reading: 1 Samuel 1:1–3:21
In-Class Reading: 1 Samuel 1:1–2:11, 18-21
Key Verses: 1 Samuel 1:27-28

Interviewer: We want to thank you, Hannah, for taking the time to be with us today. We are so honored to meet you and are anxious to hear your story—especially about young Samuel. But before we do, could you tell us a little about your background? What were your younger years like?

Hannah: Well, I grew up in an average home and had a relatively normal childhood. Like all young girls, I often dreamed of marriage and children. After all, taking care of a husband, home, and children was pretty much all we girls were trained to do. My mother spent hours teaching me everything she knew about cooking, sewing, and caring for a home and a family. The older I got, the more eager I became to get married, settle down, and start having babies to care for of my own. The day I married Elkanah was the happiest day of my life. I was finally able to start putting everything I had learned into practice, all on my own.

Interviewer: Tell me how you and Elkanah met.

Hannah: Actually, it was on one of my family's trips to Shiloh that we first met. He was traveling with his family, and I was traveling with mine. Our caravans happened onto the same path at about the same time, and it was love at first sight. I thought he was perhaps the most handsome man I had ever seen. And I was so comfortable talking with him. It was as if I had known him my entire life!

Interviewer: I guess I don't need to ask if you loved Elkanah. I can tell by your voice that the two of you were deeply in love. We've learned that too often men and women in Bible times married more for convenience. I'm glad you got to experience true love. But tell me, was there a reason why both of your families were headed to Shiloh at the same time, or was it just coincidence?

Hannah: Well, back in my day, Israelite men were required to attend religious festivals several times a year. These were usually held at the temple in Shiloh. The men didn't always take their families along with them for the journey. But this particular festival was one of special significance. It was a time set aside for the entire Israelite nation to offer sacrifices and praises to the Lord. So it wasn't uncommon for men to take their entire families along so they could celebrate as well. And that's where both our families were headed. It's possible that Elkanah and I had run into each other on earlier trips to Shiloh—we just hadn't "seen" each other, if you know what I mean!

Interviewer: Yes, I think I do. It's all in the timing and two hearts being right for each other, isn't it? Tell me, what's the story about Peninnah? I understand she was also married to Elkanah.

Hannah: Well, Elkanah and I had been married for quite some time and still hadn't had children. And since having children was of utmost importance, we agreed that Elkanah should also marry Peninnah, or "Ninah," as we nicknamed her. The only reason they married was so Elkanah could have children to carry on his family's name. It's kind of ironic: I had Elkanah's love but not his children; Ninah had his children but not his love.

Interviewer: How did you feel about that arrangement?

Hannah: Oh, at first I was OK. Now, don't get me wrong—it hurt like crazy. But I understood. It was so important to Elkanah that he have children. And it had become obvious that I was barren—that I would not be able to give him the son he wanted. But I knew he loved me. And I loved him so much. I wanted this for him as much as he wanted it. It wasn't until later on—several years later, in fact—that I began to have serious doubts about the arrangement.

Interviewer: How so?

Hannah: Well, it was Ninah. She had borne Elkanah child after child after child—both sons and daughters. There seemed to be no end to her having children. Yet, during all that time, I still hadn't had any—not one! Oh, how I prayed and prayed. All I wanted was a child—just one child! It was especially difficult when we went to Shiloh each year for our worship time. It was then that I really struggled with my emotions.

Interviewer: I guess I understand how that it would be difficult to worship and praise God as you should when it seemed he wasn't listening to you or granting you your one heart's desire.

Hannah: Actually, that wasn't the worst of it. My parents had brought me up to realize that God doesn't always give us what we ask for—or beg for, for that matter. But he would always give us exactly what we needed when we needed it. The worst of it was that when we would get to Shiloh, Ninah would line up all her children before Elkanah so he could give them—and Ninah herself—their portion of meat for the sacrifice. When that time came, it was so obvious what I didn't have—children. I stood there alone. And there she stood, with all her children, gloating over the many times the Lord had blessed her. Then she'd begin taunting me about how the Lord was not blessing me, insinuating that I was barren because the Lord God had put a curse on me.

Interviewer: I'm not sure I understand. Just because a woman isn't able to have children doesn't mean she's cursed!

Hannah: My point exactly! But in my day, that's what a lot of people thought. We all knew what a blessing children were. So, many people assumed that if you didn't have any children, it was because you had done something bad and the Lord was punishing you. But I knew the Lord loved me. I knew I hadn't done anything to deserve punishment of this kind. But it didn't lessen the sting of Ninah's words any. She could be so cruel in her remarks—sometimes without even intending to be.

Interviewer: What did Elkanah do? Surely he was aware of what was going on.

Hannah: Oh, Elkanah tried to be understanding and supportive. He really did. When he handed out the portions for the sacrifice, he always gave me a double portion and told me again how much he loved me. But he just didn't get it. Now, don't get me wrong. I loved Elkanah more than anything, and to hear him tell me again how beautiful I was and how much he loved me, well, that was wonderful. But he just didn't understand my agonizing need to have a child of my own. Know what I mean?

Interviewer: Of course I do. There are just some things that only the Lord or someone who's walked in your same shoes can understand. I've never had to deal with the agony of not being able to conceive. But I've known others who have, and I'm sure it must have been just as devastating for you back then as it is for them right now.

Hannah: Oh, it was. I often felt so useless, so lost. The more Ninah irritated and taunted me, the more depressed I became. Some days all I wanted to do was cry. Actually some days that was about the only thing I could do! During those times, I couldn't eat or sleep or even think clearly.

In fact, that's exactly what was going on during one of my most memorable trips to Shiloh. I had spent my time during supper that evening just moving food around on my plate. I was feeling so heartbroken that I couldn't eat a bite. Finally, after supper, I headed to the temple to pray. I believe I was probably at the lowest point of my life, and I thought that maybe, if I prayed to the Lord, things would get better.

Interviewer: Hannah, I don't mean to interrupt, but hadn't you been praying all along about this? Why did you think this time would be different?

Hannah: Oh, I had prayed plenty about this before, and truth be told, I don't think I really had any great expectations for a different outcome this time either. I just knew the Lord, and I knew that he was the only one I could turn to. Ninah was the cause of a lot of the heartbreak, and Elkanah didn't fully understand. Who else could I go to but the Lord?

Interviewer: Good point. So, continue on. What happened next?

Hannah: Well, by the time I got to the temple, I had been crying so hard and was so overcome with grief and anguish that the tears had stopped flowing. Words wouldn't come. I tried to speak, but all I could do was form the words with my lips and trust that the Lord knew my heart and knew what I was saying. I was in so much anguish as I prayed. You know what? I don't know if it was the grief or the anguish or what, but the words just flowed. They spilled out of me. I was praying like I had never prayed before! Usually when I prayed, although it was from my heart, it was filtered through my mind first before I spoke the words. This time, however, it seemed my prayers were taking a shortcut and going straight from my heart to God's heart. And then I heard myself praying something I'd never prayed before—and never dreamed I would pray. I vowed right then and there that if the Lord God would have favor on me and give me a son, I would give my son back to God.

Interviewer: You vowed what? Hannah, what were you thinking? How did you ever think you would be able to keep that promise—to give your baby back to God?

Hannah: Well, like I said, I was in so much agony and wanted a child in the worst way. I guess I really wasn't thinking—just praying. But after the words were out, I had no choice. Back then, if you vowed to do something, you did it. No questions asked. No backing out. At the time I had no clue if I would ever be in the situation where I would have to honor my vow. After all, I had prayed for children before and hadn't been blessed with a child. I had even prayed for a child on previous trips to the temple. Why should this time be any different?

Interviewer: But this time was different, wasn't it?

Hannah: Yes. This time was very different. I didn't know it at the time, but while I was praying, Eli the priest had been watching me. I think it's probably a good thing that I didn't know he was watching or I would have been too self-conscious. Anyway, because he didn't hear me praying out loud and only saw my lips move and my body shake from the anguish and sorrow, he thought I was drunk. So he came over to me, told me to throw away my wine, and reprimanded me for coming into the temple while I was in such a state. I was shocked that he would think such a thing! Me, Hannah, a God-fearing woman who had never even come close to doing anything like what he was accusing me of! I assured him that I was not drunk—just overcome by sadness—and that I was pouring my heart out to God. He was very understanding—here's the best part—and he said, "Cheer up! May the God of Israel grant the request you have asked of him."

Even today, I remember word for word what he said to me. I was so excited. My sadness disappeared in the blink of an eye, and I ran all the way back to the place where we were staying. I knew without a doubt the Lord had answered my prayer. I didn't know when I would see the answer. I only knew that someday I would have a child. I had never been happier.

Interviewer: Yes, but what about the vow? If you had a son, you would have to give him back to the Lord. Didn't that concern you?

Hannah: More than you'll ever know. But I also had a strange peace about it. It was almost as if I knew that when the time came, I would be strong enough to handle it.

Interviewer: So, how long did you have to wait before God answered your prayer?

Hannah: Actually, not long at all. Early the next morning, the whole family got up and went to worship one last time before heading back home to Ramah. Once we got back home and Elkanah and I had some time alone, I told Elkanah what had happened to me that last night at the temple. I told him everything—my anguish and desperation, my sorrow, my prayer, and my answer through Eli the priest.

Interviewer: What was his reaction? Was he as convinced as you were that the Lord was going to answer your prayer?

Hannah: I'm not sure. Let's just say he was mildly optimistic. He wanted it to be true—for me, more so than for himself. But I think he was afraid I was setting myself up for more disappointment.

Interviewer: Didn't you ever feel a tinge of doubt—that maybe having a child was never meant to be for you?

Hannah: Before, maybe. But not after talking with Eli! After he said what he did to me, I just knew in my heart that my prayer was going to be answered. The only thing that surprised me, really, was how quickly it all came about! You know, we had not been back to Ramah very long before I began to suspect I might be pregnant. Then, as the months passed, it wasn't just my belly that grew, but also my praise and adoration for such a loving and caring God. After all these years, he had seen fit to shower me with the blessing of a child. I could not praise him enough.

Interviewer: How did Elkanah and Ninah react to your condition?

Hannah: Oh, as you can guess, Ninah wasn't happy at all. She knew of Elkanah's love for me, and as long as she was the one bearing him children, she thought maybe she would eventually gain the upper hand and become his favorite.

But Elkanah—oh, you couldn't have asked for a better, more supportive husband. He was so attentive. As soon as he knew, he began treating me like royalty. He waited on me hand and foot and saw that others did the same. I'm sure he was afraid I might miscarry, but I had no fear of that. I knew in my heart this was the Lord's answer. I knew, at long last, I would have a child.

Interviewer: But still, what about the vow? I can't help but think that had to worry you and take away some of your joy.

Hannah: Not at all. Concern, maybe. But never worry. It's hard to explain, and I really don't expect you to understand, but I truly had peace. If I had a son, I knew the Lord would be with me and would help me be strong when the time came to give my baby back to him. Then, when Samuel was born, I became convinced all the more that the Lord would help me. I realized there was no way I would be able to do it on my own. I had to rely on him for my strength.

Interviewer: How did you come to name him Samuel?

Hannah: Well, I thought long and hard about it. I wanted a name that clearly portrayed my feelings and yet also told his story. I chose the name Samuel because it means "Asked of the Lord." It seemed to fit our circumstances perfectly—I had asked the Lord for him, and the Lord God had answered.

Interviewer: That it does. Tell me a bit about Samuel's early years. What was he like?

Hannah: Oh, he was very special, of course! Being my only child, I protected him with every ounce of strength I had. And Elkanah, well, he doted on him like you wouldn't believe. Samuel was a very special gift from the Lord. He was so delightful. He seemed to be so alert and advanced for his age, too. He seemed to understand things that were hard for me to comprehend. And smart, oh, he was smart! I spent those early years enjoying every minute with him.

Interviewer: How did you tell Samuel about your vow?

Hannah: That was hard. But from day one I had told Samuel how he came to be and how special he was. I made sure he understood the meaning behind his name and what the Lord intended for his life.

Then, when Samuel was about two and it was time for the yearly sacrifice, I didn't go. Instead, I sent Elkanah, Ninah, and all the rest of the family on to Shiloh without Samuel and me. I promised Elkanah that the next year, when Samuel was three, I would make the trip and would turn Samuel over to Eli for service to the Lord God.

Interviewer: How did Elkanah feel? I'm sure the thought of giving up Samuel was just as hard for him.

Hannah: Oh, I'm sure it was. But he also knew how important it was for me to keep my vow. Before leaving for Shiloh that year without me, he said, "May the Lord help you keep your promise." That's when I knew how concerned he was. He never said so, but I suspect his prayer time at the temple that year was spent in large part praying not only for me but also for Samuel and our last year together as a family—that I would have the courage and strength to give back to the Lord this precious gift.

Interviewer: I imagine your last year with Samuel went by much too quickly.

Hannah: Did it ever! I prayed and cried myself to sleep more nights than I could count. When Elkanah told me that it was time to prepare to go to Shiloh again, I couldn't believe our final year with Samuel was already over. It seemed like just yesterday that they were all returning from last year's trip!

But it was time. It was so hard to pack for that trip. I treasured everything of Samuel's as I put it in his bag, and I prayed almost constantly. I think his bag was as full of my tears as it was of anything else. I knew I would be facing by far the hardest thing in my life.

Interviewer: Hannah, I cannot imagine facing what you faced. How did you ever do it? How were you ever able to turn Samuel over to Eli?

Hannah: Well, the days it took us to travel from Ramah to Shiloh were the longest of my life. All I could do was put one step in front of the other. With each step, I knew I was that much closer to the inevitable. I knew I had prepared both Samuel and myself as best I knew how. I just hoped it was enough.

The evening we stepped through the city gate at Shiloh, the sun was just setting. I thought how appropriate that was. Our life with Samuel as we knew it was coming to an end. Tomorrow would be the day.

Interviewer: I'll bet you didn't sleep a wink that night.

Hannah: Actually, I didn't. I was reminded of a previous trip to Shiloh—the one when I begged God for Samuel. Like that night, I could neither eat nor sleep. Tears of anguish just flowed down my cheeks. And just like before, by the time I got to the temple the next morning, my tears were all cried out. But unlike the last time, I was able to think and speak clearly.

After sacrificing a 3-year-old bull, Elkanah and I each took one of Samuel's tiny little 3-year-old hands and walked straight to Eli the priest. Elkanah and Eli allowed me to speak and tell our story. I reminded Eli of the time we had met and told him what my prayer had been that day and how the Lord had answered through him. I told him of the vow and how I was ready to fulfill my part by turning Samuel over to the Lord for service in the temple.

With deep understanding in his eyes, Eli bent down and took Samuel's hand, and the two of them began talking. As Elkanah and I were walking away, we turned and took one last look at our baby. What we saw—Eli and Samuel together praising God—both comforted and blessed us. Our hearts, although broken, were at peace.

Interviewer: Hannah, you've nearly got me in tears! You are such a remarkable woman. Even though we're about out of time, I would like to hear more of your story. Please, continue.

Hannah: Well, before Elkanah and I even got out the temple door, I couldn't help but praise the Lord myself. He had given me the delight of my heart through Samuel, and now, even after all we had just been through, I again found myself rejoicing. I discovered a different kind of delight—one that comes from full obedience to God.

The trip home was still long, but my heart was at peace. I knew without a doubt I had done what the Lord expected of me.

And every year from then on, when I went to the temple for our yearly sacrifices, I took along a robe I had made for Samuel. And every year, Eli would say a special blessing over us and would pray that the Lord would bless us with more children.

Interviewer: Did he?

Hannah: Oh, my goodness, yes! I ended up having three more boys and two girls—blessings each and every one. But as you can guess, a big chunk of my heart always stayed with Samuel.

Interviewer: Hannah, what a magnificent story. And what a testimony you have! In looking back over your life, what would you say were the most important lessons you learned?

Hannah: I think one would have to be that of trusting God and being obedient to him. Sometimes we may be asked to turn over our most precious treasures to him. In my case, it was my child. For others, it might be something entirely different. It might be a special relationship or a dream you've had for a long, long time. I learned that if you let go of it with a heart that truly trusts the Lord, he will fill the void with a joy you could not have thought or imagined.

Another lesson is to not be afraid to tell God exactly how you feel. Even though he already knows, he wants to know that you love him enough to share everything with him. He wants you to be honest and open with him about absolutely everything—the good, the bad, and the ugly.

Interviewer: Hannah, thank you so much for joining us. We have enjoyed visiting with you and have truly been blessed by your testimony. Thank you so much.

DISCUSSION QUESTIONS:

1. Hannah was asked to turn over her precious 3-year-old son to God. And as unfathomable as it may seem, she did it with grace and dignity. Have you ever had to turn something precious over to the Lord? If so, what was it, and how hard was that for you to do?

2. Just as in Bible times, we know that children are a gift from God. Our role as Christian parents is to nurture, train, and lead them to a point where we release them over to service for God, to do what he has planned for them. How is what we are asked to do with our children different from or similar to what Hannah was asked to do?

3. Hannah's inability to bear children caused a lot of heartache in her life. People in Bible times assumed her barrenness was punishment for some grievous sin she had committed. Others, like Peninnah, taunted her. How are childless women today treated differently from the way they were in Bible times? How are they treated similarly?

4. Have you ever prayed for something for a long time and God just didn't seem to be listening? If so, has God answered that prayer, or are you still waiting? If you're still in God's "waiting room," how can you be sure what you're praying is in accordance with God's will?

5. Hannah found herself praying one of those "If you'll do this, God, then I'll do this" prayers. Have you ever prayed one of those "if-then" prayers? If so, has God taken you up on it?

6. Hannah encourages us to be completely open and honest with God in our prayers. Why is that often so hard to do?

Miriam

Background Reading: Exodus 1:6–2:10; 15:20-
21; Numbers 12:1-15; 20:1
In-Class Reading: Exodus 1:6-2:10; Numbers
12:1-15
Key Verse: Exodus 2:4

Interviewer: Welcome to our class, Miriam. It is so nice
to have you join us today. We have been anxious to
meet you and to learn more about your story. Our
first—and probably favorite—story about you is the
one when you were a young girl hiding out near the
Nile River. Would you mind telling us about that?

Miriam: You know, I think that story is a favorite among
a lot of people. And although it was many, many
years ago, in some ways it seems as if it happened
yesterday. I remember the morning I woke up to the
sound of Mom sobbing. I couldn't imagine what had
gotten her so upset. Everything had seemed all right
the night before. So, I got up and began to quietly—
and gingerly, I might add—walk into her room. Dad
met me just inside the door and told me that the baby
had been born. A boy. That was all he needed to say
for me to understand. You see, they really wanted a

baby girl. And so did I. I wanted a baby sister more than just about anything. After all, I already had a baby brother—what did I need another one of those for? What I really needed was a sister!

Interviewer: I can understand why you would want a sister, but why didn't your parents want a boy? I thought back in your day most people wanted sons.

Miriam: Oh, they did. Sons were important. Sons grew up and became men with families of their own who carried on the family name. Daughters grew up to become wives and mothers to others. In a lot of cases, we girls were really not considered much more important than another piece of property.

Come to think about it, during that time in Israel's history, we were all pretty much considered pieces of property—all of us Israelites, that is. We had been in Egypt long enough that our ancestors, Joseph and all his brothers, had died, and a new Pharaoh had come into power. This new king of Egypt didn't know (or didn't care—I'm not sure which) about Joseph and all he had done—especially with regard to saving the whole nation during a famine. Instead, all Pharaoh saw was a bunch of Israelites multiplying like crazy in "his" country.

I guess he saw us as a threat to taking over some day. Anyway, one of the first things he did was turn us into slaves, thinking that would keep us from having so many babies. I remember my dad coming home from work so tired and exhausted. Mom would rub his shoulders, trying to relax his tense, sore muscles. And many nights, he would fall asleep almost before supper was over. I felt so sorry for him. I would hear Mom and Dad talk about a better life. Oh, how they longed to have a life of freedom! They often told Aaron, my brother, and me stories about how life used to be before slavery. It sounded so wonderful. But instead of things getting better, they only got worse. Then, shortly after Mom found out she was going to have another baby, Pharaoh declared, "Enough is enough!" He decided that if the Israelites could not or would not stop having children, he would do something about Israel's growth spurt once and for all. So, he commanded that the midwives kill all the Israelite boys the minute they were born. But the midwives were God-fearing women. They couldn't do that any more than you or I could kill a baby. Well, when Pharaoh found out his latest plan wasn't working, he went even further and demanded that all the newborn Israelite boys be thrown into the Nile River and left to drown. So, you can see now why Mom and Dad wanted a baby girl.

Interviewer: Oh, of course. My goodness, I hadn't realized how hard things had gotten for you and your family. Tell me, what did your parents do when they saw they had a baby boy?

Miriam: Oh, they agonized for days over what to do. They knew they had to do everything they could to keep him safe. I guess they were thinking—hoping— that the Israelites would somehow be set free before he was found out.

Anyway, Mom and Dad knew their life had to remain as normal as possible so it wouldn't appear as if they were hiding something. So, that morning Dad headed off to make bricks as usual, and Mom got up and did her normal activities. I cannot imagine how hard it must have been for her after just giving birth, but she did it. In so many ways, my mom taught me what strength was. You just do what you have to do, when you have to do it. And if you rely on God, he will help you through it, no matter what the situation is.

Well, we lived like that for quite a while—the usual routine for the four of us—Mom, Dad, Aaron, and me. When Mom went to the market, she would leave me in charge of my baby brother—Moses, as he came to be known later on. We kept him hidden in the house, and the minute he even whimpered, we would do whatever we could to keep him quiet—give him something to eat, change him, hold him—anything and everything just so he'd stay quiet!

We lived like that for weeks. Then, when my brother was about three months old, Mom and Dad realized they could not hide him much longer. Each day he seemed to get louder and louder and more and more active. They knew it was just a matter of time before they were going to be found out and he would be thrown into the river like the other baby boys. So one night they decided to waterproof a basket. And the next morning, after Dad headed off to work, Mom wrapped the baby in a blanket and put him in the basket. Then, the two of us—Mom and I—went to the river where Mom carefully placed the basket among the reeds along the water's edge.

Interviewer: Oh, Miriam, that had to have been so hard for her. I just can't imagine how desperate she must have been. So, tell us, what happened next?

Miriam: Well, we had purposely taken him to an area of the river where we knew Pharaoh's daughter bathed. So, Mom prayed that she—Pharaoh's daughter—

would be the one to find him and that she would be kind and merciful toward him.

Interviewer: But I thought it was Pharaoh who was having all the Israelite babies killed. What made your mom think his daughter would act kindly toward an Israelite baby?

Miriam: I think Mom felt as if this was her only choice. If another one of the Israelite women had found him, he would have been discovered and killed just as he certainly would have been had he remained with us. If one of the Egyptian women found him, what chance did she have of keeping an Israelite baby once Pharaoh found out? But the princess—well, everyone knew Pharaoh doted on her. If anyone could sweet-talk him into not killing one of the Israelite babies, it was her. Mom actually saw her as the only chance she had of keeping her baby alive.

Interviewer: I guess that makes sense. So, what happened next, after you put the basket in the reeds?

Miriam: Well, Mom couldn't stand to be there any longer. Besides, if anyone saw her, they would have wondered why she was hanging around there—that was something we kids did. So, Mom went back home while I was instructed to keep a close eye on the basket and let her know what happened. So I did. I was so nervous. And it seemed like I was there for *so* long, although I'm sure now it couldn't have been more than an hour or two. Then, finally, I saw the princess. I must admit, I was excited at first. It was like I was playing a sort of spy game. But then, it began to embarrass me that I was watching her every move because she was, after all, there to bathe. Which, by the way, I always thought was odd. Why didn't she just take a bath back at the palace? Surely she had a place there where she could bathe with a lot more privacy. Anyway, I watched—and watched closely, mind you. After all, the princess was so close to the basket!

Then she saw it. That's when I began to hold my breath! What would she do? What would she think? A million thoughts ran through my mind. Then I began to think, what if she saw me hiding, spying on her? Would she be mad? Would I get in trouble? How do I get out of this predicament? About that time, Pharaoh's daughter called for her servant girl to get the basket. That's when I knew I had the chance to make a move. So I came out from hiding and inched closer, making my presence known. I acted as if I was just a curious little Israelite girl out playing. The princess saw me but didn't say anything at first. I remember thinking I had gotten away with being a spy. But in retrospect, I wonder if all along she suspected who I was—the baby's sister. But I'm getting ahead of myself. Let me back up a bit in my story.

I knew the princess could hear my baby brother crying before she even looked inside the basket. In fact, I could hear him even where I was! He did have a set of lungs! But I still didn't know what kind of person the princess was. As it turned out, she fell in love with him the minute she saw him. And she suspected how he came to be in the river. She knew that there was some mother out there who saw this as her last hope to keep her son alive. And I think it melted her heart. Anyway, I heard her tell her servant girl that she was of half a mind to keep him herself, but that she had a problem—he was too young and still needed to be nursed. When I heard that, I finally approached her and offered to get a Hebrew woman to nurse him for her. She thought that was the perfect solution and asked me to go get someone for her. And of course, I headed straight home to get Mom! I ran as fast as my little legs would carry me.

Interviewer: How did your mom react when you told her about what had happened and what she was being asked to do?

Miriam: Well, as you can guess, I was so excited I burst through the door. I found Mom sitting in the corner next to the baby's things. But I didn't lose a beat. Even before my feet stopped, my mouth started talking. I'm really surprised Mom could understand a word I said, I was talking so fast. Anyway, Mom was stunned at the turn of events. This was beyond her wildest dreams. So she ran back with me to the princess, both of us hoping against hope that she would still be there with our baby.

Interviewer: Was she?

Miriam: She was! Oh, it was absolutely wonderful. The princess asked Mom if she would be willing to nurse Moses—for pay, of course—until he was weaned. Moses. That was the name she gave him. It means "to draw out." Appropriate, don't you think? Anyway, it was like a dream come true. Not only did we get Moses back, but Mom also got paid to care for him! Isn't it amazing how God can turn things around so completely? And to do it in the space of only a couple of hours! My mom went from devastating sorrow to overwhelming joy that morning.

Interviewer: Yes, it truly is amazing what God can do. I'll venture to say that those few years you had with Moses went by much too quickly.

Miriam: Oh, did they ever! We were so happy to be a complete family. Daddy had hurried home from work that day expecting to find the worst. Instead, imagine his surprise to find the son he'd thought he'd lost! And oh, the story Mom had to tell! I'm not sure Mom or Dad ever got to the point where they fully understood how compassionate God is. But then again, I'm not sure any of us do. We try, but there is no way our feeble minds can understand the depth of his love.

Anyway, it was such a relief not to have to hide Moses any longer! Now Mom could take him with her everywhere she went. But that presented another whole set of problems.

Interviewer: How so?

Miriam: Well, we had to be careful around the other women who had lost their sons at the hand of Pharaoh. We had to be understanding and sensitive to their feelings as well.

Interviewer: I hadn't thought about that. But you're right. That had to have been quite a balancing act.

Miriam: Oh, it was. But as time passed, things began to get easier.

Interviewer: So, how did the next few years play out? Did Pharaoh's daughter keep in touch during those years?

Miriam: Actually, she did. She always made sure Moses was cared for and had everything he needed. And Mom and Dad saw to it that he learned about his own family history as well. It seemed that every time we turned around, they were telling us stories about our ancestors—especially how we got to be in Egypt in the first place and how, someday, we would leave. Mom and Dad always knew that eventually the Israelites would get back to their homeland. They just didn't know when—or how—it would happen. Mom would tell stories and sing favorite songs all the time—while she nursed Moses, while we played together, ate together, before going to bed. She and Dad took every opportunity to instill in us a love for God. They also let us know that there was nothing God couldn't handle or take care of. I could not have asked for better parents.

Interviewer: I'd have to agree with you. Your parents must have been fabulous. They did rear three children who all became outstanding and exceptional adults. Tell us, what happened next?

Miriam: Well, the day we all had dreaded finally came, and we had to give Moses up.

Interviewer: You know, Miriam, I hate to interrupt, but your story sounds so familiar. We were talking with Hannah not too long ago, and she told us the story of how she had to give up Samuel, her young son. That was after your lifetime, but like Hannah, I'm sure this was not an easy thing for your parents to do. I hadn't really thought about the fact that your mom had to give Moses up twice—once in the basket as an infant and again to live in Pharaoh's palace with the princess. That had to be such an incredibly hard thing for her to do.

Miriam: It was. After that point, we only saw Moses occasionally. But he always greeted us so warmly. Mom had prepared him for this time, so he knew that this was God's will for his life, even though none of us understood why. It was many years later before we began to see how God's plan was unfolding. Meanwhile, Mom, Dad, Aaron, and I all watched from a distance. On the one hand, Mom and Dad were proud of him; on the other, they worried that he would forget his roots. On the one hand, Aaron and I adored him; on the other, we found ourselves becoming jealous of him.

Interviewer: What caused you and Aaron such jealousy?

Miriam: Well, it was lots of things, actually. It just seemed as if he lived a life of privilege and stardom. He always seemed to be front and center, and that bothered us. He grew up in Pharaoh's palace; we grew up working our fingers to the bone as slaves. He grew up dressed in the finest clothes; we were lucky to get a new robe or sandals every couple of years. He ate the richest of foods; we ate the same old boring, tasteless food. And the biggie? Well, it's another long story, but even after Moses had killed a man, ran off to the land of Midian to escape punishment, and married a foreigner, God still chose him to lead our people out of Egypt! To top it all off, Moses was already 80 years old by that time! Aaron and I—and a lot of other people, mind you—couldn't understand God's thinking. Wouldn't someone 20 or 30 years younger have been the wiser choice? And besides that, as much as we loved Moses, he wasn't a leader by any stretch of the imagination! And you know, Moses didn't see himself as a leader, either. When God told him what he was to do, the first thing Moses did was beg God to send someone else. But God had already planned for Moses to be the one to rescue the Israelites from the Egyptians. So, instead of sending someone else to do the job, God reluctantly agreed to allow Aaron to be Moses' spokesman. And the two of them began working together to bring about God's deliverance of the Hebrews. So, in essence, Aaron became Moses' megaphone, telling the people what Moses told him to. However, Moses still called all the shots. He was the one who got to meet and talk with God through the burning bush. He was the one who got to climb Mt. Sinai again and again to meet and talk directly with God. It was always Moses. He seemed to be God's center of attention, and Aaron and I seemed to be in God's periphery.

Interviewer: My, you do sound a little jealous!

Miriam: I know. And I'm sorry about that. But I'm just telling it the way it was. I did have an awful time adjusting to his authority. After all, he was my younger brother! It took me years, but I did finally get accustomed to taking orders from him. But that didn't come without some moments of outright rebellion and resentment on my part. It's a wonder God put up with me!

Interviewer: My goodness, Miriam, what kind of things did you do?

Miriam: Well, I think it was as much what I didn't do as it was what I did do. For instance, what I didn't do was realize—or rather, accept—the fact that Moses was God's choice in leading the people out of Egypt. I had known Moses from the day he was born and saw how human he was and the mistakes he had made. I had trouble believing that God would choose someone like him to accomplish this humongous task. I guess it was all a little too hard for me to believe. Am I making any sense at all?

Interviewer: Yes, I think it's hard for any close family member of anyone who becomes a "celebrity" to accept that fact. After all, you've grown up with them; you've seen their mistakes and their faults. But honestly, Miriam, in what I've read about you, it seems God had called you into a leadership position of your own. It wasn't just Moses or Aaron. You had a vital role as well.

Miriam: I suppose I did. But early on I didn't realize it. I guess I was too focused on Moses and what God was doing through him. At the time I couldn't see what God might have in mind for me to do or how he was at work in my life.

Interviewer: Miriam, could you share with us just how you came to realize and understand the role God intended for you?

Miriam: Oh, how I wish I could say I was a quick learner! But I wasn't. As soon as God set into motion his plan for our deliverance, one thing after another happened that always left me questioning God even more.

Interviewer: Like what kind of things?

Miriam: Well, one of the first things God expected Moses to do was to get permission from Pharaoh for the Hebrews to leave the country. Moses knew that would not be easy. After all, we had been Pharaoh's slaves and major brick-builders for many, many years! He wasn't about to let the cheap labor go. But God—and Moses—were determined. I do have to give Moses credit for that!

Anyway, time after time, Moses and Aaron approached Pharaoh requesting permission to leave Egypt for a brief time so we could worship as a nation. But time after time, Pharaoh refused. And every time he refused, God sent a plague on the entire country— ten of them in all! It was downright awful. You name it, we had it—blood, frogs, gnats, flies, boils, hail, locusts—we had them all and more! Actually, some of the plagues didn't affect the Israelites at all—only the Egyptians. But we could see and hear their agony. I always felt so sorry for the innocent Egyptians. A lot of them actually looked up to Moses and had great respect for him. They had to endure so much because of Pharaoh. He was so stubborn that finally what it took was a plague of death. We Israelites had been forewarned, so we knew to mark our doors. And about midnight one night, it happened. The firstborn of all the Egyptians were instantly killed—from the Pharaoh's own palace to the Egyptian slaves, even to the livestock. Well, that was the last straw, and Pharaoh finally gave up. He immediately called for Moses and Aaron and demanded we leave!

Well, he didn't need to say it twice! Moses had told us the day before to prepare to travel, so we were already pretty much ready to go. And as we were leaving the country, we had been told to ask the Egyptians for silver, gold, and clothing. Which, by the way, they were more than willing to give! They were so eager to have us gone. They had realized, much sooner than Pharaoh, that all the plagues and problems they had been having were because of us. So, they wanted to be rid of us as soon as possible. We actually began marching out of Egypt even before daylight!

Interviewer: You must have been so relieved—and excited—to finally be rid of Pharaoh and the living conditions in Egypt.

Miriam: Yes, we were. But as excited as we were, it wasn't long before we began to have serious doubts about leaving. More than once, people actually wanted to turn back. Things got pretty bad at times.

Interviewer: How so?

Miriam: That's another long story—actually some 40 years worth! But I'll try to condense it a bit.

Interviewer: I'm sure we'd all appreciate that! After all, we are almost out of time!

Miriam: Well, as you can imagine, it took several days for all of us to get out of Egypt. After all, there was a good bit of walking involved, and there were a million or so of us! However, once we were away from Egypt's borders, we expected God to take us on a direct route to our Promised Land. But he didn't! Instead, we headed through the wilderness toward the Red Sea. That's when the murmurings really began in earnest. We were all questioning Moses as to why we were taking the long way around—especially given the number of women and children in the group. But Moses assured us that this was God's idea—not his—and that everything would be OK. During that time, we experienced a lot of tense situations. But God always seemed to come to our rescue at the last minute, with miracle after miracle, in spite of all our whining.

Interviewer: What kind of miracles are you talking about?

Miriam: Well, like providing a cloud for us to follow each day and a pillar of fire at night; walking through the Red Sea on dry ground; receiving bread straight from heaven's oven and water from a rock; winning a battle just because Moses kept his arms raised. That was a biggie! After our victory, Moses led the people in a song of praise, and then I grabbed my tambourine and led all the women in rhythm and dance. It was really quite a celebration! But it didn't last. Even with all the miracles, we Israelites kept complaining. We were tired of camping out, and many times we begged to go back to Egypt. You know, sometimes I think I was the worst complainer of all!

Interviewer: What did you do that was any worse than what the others did?

Miriam: Well, one particularly embarrassing incident stands out in my mind. Remember, we had been on the road for years. We were tired—all of us! One day Aaron and I were especially out of sorts and the two of us began criticizing Moses about his choice of wives. Then we began to feed each others' egos with reminders of how God had also used us during our wanderings—acting as if we were just as important as Moses.

Interviewer: Oh, Miriam, what were the two of you thinking?

Miriam: We were so tired and frustrated that we hadn't stopped to think that God could hear us. But he did. And boy, was he mad! God immediately called us on the carpet. He told all three of us to go into the portable tabernacle. Then he came down in the form of a cloud and blocked the entrance so we couldn't get out. He called Aaron and me forward and straightened us out about who was who, once and for all. God left no doubt as to who he wanted in charge, and it wasn't either one of us! And then, as if to emphasize what he said, he caused me to get leprosy. I turned white as a sheet. Aaron began begging for forgiveness from Moses; Moses began begging for mercy for me and my healing. So God told Moses to banish me from the camp for seven days, and then I could return.

Interviewer: What did you do during those seven days?

Miriam: I did a lot of thinking and praying, believe me! Even though it was hard and I hated it, it was probably the best thing for me. It was during this time that I settled in my mind who was in charge and what my role had been all along.

Interviewer: And what exactly had your role been?

Miriam: Well, to my surprise, I discovered that it had been the same role that I'd had back when Moses was a baby in the Nile River. My job was to support Moses by standing at a distance and seeing what would happen. My job was to encourage him and stand by his decisions, trusting that God was at work through him.

Interviewer: Miriam, I really hate to do this, but it is past time for us to be winding up this interview. I think you have done an outstanding job summarizing your life. Your life certainly was interesting and full of ups and downs! Before we close, I'd like to ask you what we've asked every other woman who's joined us—"What lessons did you learn from your life that we would do well to learn?"

Miriam: Well, I guess that I learned there are no small roles in God's plan. Learn what it is God expects you to do and strive to do it to the best of your ability.

I would also advise you to accept and support those whom God places in authority over you. Believe me, I wasted a lot of years before wholeheartedly accepting Moses' authority. But in the end, I became one of his biggest fans!

Lastly, I would say I learned to back off and allow God the freedom to work in his own way and time. That's part of what the seven days taught me. For seven days, the Israelites—and Moses—managed without me and my input. It was hard for me to accept, but I learned that things turned out a whole lot better when I stepped back and let God take over.

Interviewer: Miriam, thank you so much for joining us. You have really been a delight—and such a blessing! Thank you.

DISCUSSION QUESTIONS:

1. Miriam speaks so lovingly of her mother and her strength and belief in God. One of the lessons her mother taught her was that if she relied on God, he would help her through any situation or problem that came up. If you grew up in a Christian home, what lessons about God did your mother pass on to you?

2. One thing Miriam noticed as a young girl was how quickly God can turn a situation around. In just a short time, she saw her mother go from extreme sorrow to extreme joy. Have you ever had a situation in which your emotions plummeted and then skyrocketed at such amazing speeds that it left you in awe of God?

3. Early on, Miriam gave Moses credit for his persistence in approaching Pharaoh. Have you ever been persistent in a situation? If so, in looking back, are you 100 percent sure it was God's will that you persist?

4. Miriam noted through the wilderness wanderings that God doesn't always work in the way that seems best to us. Have you ever been in a situation when you wondered just why God was leading you in the direction he was? Why do you think God will often take people on the "scenic route" instead of the shortcut?

5. Miriam suggested there may have been several reasons why God sent her on a seven-day "retreat." What are some reasons you can think of?

6. As Christians, we are all God's representatives. Miriam learned the hard way that there are no small roles in God's plan. We each have a unique part we are

expected to fulfill. What role—or roles—do you feel God has assigned you in order to further his plans?

Esther

Background Reading: Esther 1–10
In-Class Reading: Esther 5:3–7:10
Key Verses: 4:14-16

Interviewer: Queen Esther, we are so very honored and humbled that you would take the time to join us. You'll have to excuse me if I stammer a little, but I've never been in the presence of a real live queen before! It is such a thrill and joy to have royalty visiting us.

Esther: Oh, please, please don't think of me as royalty. That was only my "position in life"—a position I seemed destined to have in order to fulfill what God intended me to do. I'm just like any other woman, with the same feelings and emotions that you have.

Interviewer: Thank you, Queen Esther. You've reminded me of a lesson we women tend to forget—we're all pretty much the same. Oh, our appearances and experiences in life may vary, but deep down we all have similar hopes and dreams for our lives and our families. And we have all experienced sorrow as well as joy. Sometimes we tend to think that the more popular or well-known a woman is, the greater or more worthy she is. But that's just not the case. Did you run into that stereotyping back in your day?

Esther: Yes, we sure did. And while we're at it, let's drop the "queen" stuff. Just call me Esther, OK?

Interviewer: OK, Esther it is. Esther, what was your childhood like?

Esther: Well, my childhood was a bit rough in that I lost both of my parents early on in life. I only vaguely remember them. But I had a wonderful, caring older cousin who took me in and took care of me as if I was his own daughter.

Years earlier, my people—the Jews—had been taken into captivity and were exiled to Persia. And even though we later gained our freedom and could have gone back to Jerusalem, Mordecai, my cousin, chose to stay. And since he was now my guardian, I stayed, which is how I ended up being in Persia during the time King Xerxes was searching for a new queen.

Interviewer: Why was he looking for a new queen? What happened to the one he had?

Esther: Well, her name was Queen Vashti, and rumor has it that she refused an official order of the king. He had just spent six months partying and drinking with all the nobles and officials and was busy showing off his vast wealth. Then, after showing off all his valuable possessions, the king asked Queen Vashti to make an appearance and join him and his partying friends so he could show off her beauty. She refused. She may have refused in part because she was throwing a banquet for the women and didn't want to leave her guests. But I think the main reason she didn't go was because she knew King Xerxes and his friends had been partying and drinking for months on end and would be drunk. And that was the last situation any woman wanted to place herself in. So, she didn't go.

Interviewer: I'll bet that sent some rumbling throughout the palace corridors!

Esther: You bet it did! King Xerxes was furious! He immediately consulted with all his advisors, and to make a long story short, Queen Vashti was thrown out of there quicker than anything. It seems all the bigwigs thought that what Queen Vashti had done would trickle down through the ranks, and before you knew it, women everywhere would start disobeying their husbands. You need to understand that in my day, submission on the wife's part was not only expected—it was demanded. For Vashti to do such a thing, especially in her position, shocked the whole Persian Empire.

Interviewer: So how did you come to be in the palace?

Esther: Well, after King Xerxes cooled down a bit, he realized what a rash—and poor—decision he had made. After all, what kind of a king didn't have a queen in the palace, ready to stand by his side and do his bidding? He had to keep up appearances, you know. But he couldn't go back on what he had said. There was no way he could take Queen Vashti back. After all, how would that look? Any decree he made from that point on would have been looked upon as negotiable. People would always wonder if he really meant what he said. So, he felt as if he had to stick to his own orders—even if they were made in the heat of the moment. Xerxes found himself caught between a rock and a hard place. He didn't have a queen, and he couldn't reinstate Vashti. So he decided to have the most beautiful women in Persia brought into his harem, with the intention of finding a replacement queen from among them.

Interviewer: And you were one of them.

Esther: Yes. I was chosen as one of them. Even though I wasn't Persian, I had lived in Persia my entire life, so everyone thought I was. And when I was selected, I didn't tell them any differently.

Interviewer: Why not?

Esther: I wasn't sure why at the time. Cousin Mordecai had told me not to. And since I trusted him completely, I didn't question him—I only did what he said. In retrospect, I'm sure it was God who had laid it on his heart that this bit of news needed to remain a secret from the palace officials.

Interviewer: What happened once you were taken to the palace?

Esther: Well, as I said, I was put in a harem with a lot of other young women and was placed under the care of Hegai. He was the eunuch in charge of my beauty treatments.

Interviewer: Beauty treatments? I thought you were there because you were already beautiful.

Esther: So they said. I never thought of myself that way at all. So, this was all pretty new to me. I learned that it was customary for any woman who was to be presented to the king to go through a whole year's worth of beauty treatments first. I personally thought that was a bit extravagant. Anyway, it was assumed that you were there in the harem of the king because you were vying to become the next queen.

Interviewer: Weren't you?

Esther: Others were. I wasn't. Actually, I wasn't sure why I was there. I really had no thought of ever being queen. Everything seemed to happen so suddenly, and I was just going with the flow. At first I felt as if I was caught up in a whirlwind. Then, when the beauty treatments began, my life seemed to come to a halt. All of a sudden, now I was spending long, boring days being rubbed down with oil. There wasn't much for us girls to talk about. After all, we were pretty much secluded and protected from the outside world. So, day in, day out, I sat there listening to the other girls gush and swoon over the king and talk about how they hoped they would be the chosen one. That went on for six long months! Then, after that, I spent another six months undergoing special treatments with perfumes and ointments, listening to more of the same jibber-jabber. I was nearly bored out of my mind! Maybe things would have been different if I'd had the lofty goal they had. The other girls didn't seem to mind the excessive pampering at all—probably because they were so hopeful to be the next

"Mrs. Xerxes." But that was the farthest thing from my mind. All I could think was, "What in the world am I doing here?" I was so homesick.

Interviewer: I'm sure that must have been a lonely time for you. Did you get to see your family during this time?

Esther: During that first year, I heard from Mordecai occasionally. But I saw no one else. Shortly after I became queen, Mordecai became a palace official, so then I got to hear from him with some regularity. But other than that, my life was pretty much secluded.

Interviewer: Let's backtrack for just a moment. Could you tell us about how you were selected to be the next queen?

Esther: Well, there's not much to tell. It was just another one of those whirlwind experiences I always seemed to find myself getting caught up in. After the year of pampering was over, I was presented to the king. The next thing I knew, the crown was placed on my head, and a big banquet was thrown in my honor. I could not believe the king had chosen me over all the other girls. I didn't know what to do. I'd obviously never been a queen before. How was I supposed to act? What was required of me? So many questions kept dashing through my brain. But as it turned out, I didn't need to worry about any of them.

Interviewer: Why not?

Esther: Because just as suddenly as it all happened, it stopped. I was dismissed until the king called for me again. Just like that! One minute I was the center of attention, and the next minute it seemed I'd been put in storage—only to be taken out again if and when the king called for me. So my life went back to boring. But you know, I came to appreciate the boring days—especially after my next whirlwind experience!

Interviewer: Why? What happened then?

Esther: Well, as I hear you all say, "Drama . . . drama . . . drama!" It all began when King Xerxes promoted a man named Haman to be prime minister. That, in essence, made him the second most powerful official in the entire empire of Persia. Haman was a man with a big head. He had manipulated Xerxes to declare that all the other officials in the palace were to bow down to him just as they did in the presence of the king. And they did—except for my cousin Mordecai, that is. When Mordecai was questioned about his refusal to bow before Haman, he said it was because he was a Jew. This made Haman furious. In fact, he was so mad that he plotted to have all the Jews in the empire killed. Of course, key to the success of this mission was the king himself. So, Haman went to Xerxes and told him that there was a race of people living in Persia who refused to obey the king's laws. Then he urged King Xerxes to see to it that these people were destroyed. Haman even bribed Xerxes, saying that if the king would do him this one favor, he would give lots of money to the treasury. So, King Xerxes, without bothering to look into the matter, handed over his royal seal to Haman, giving him authority to make decrees on behalf of the king. Well, the first thing Haman did was turn around and dictate letters stating that by the time one year had passed, every Jew in Persia was to be killed.

Well, when Mordecai got wind of this, he went into a state of deep mourning for the Jews in Persia. He tore his clothes, put on sackcloth and ashes, and began crying and wailing.

Interviewer: How did you find out about what was going on?

Esther: One of my maids came and told me about Mordecai. I didn't know why he was in mourning. So I sent him a fresh set of clothes, because most people who mourned also tore at their clothes in grief. But he refused to accept them. Anyway, because Mordecai refused the clothes, I sent one of the king's eunuchs to find out what was going on. Well, Mordecai showed him a copy of the decree. Then he asked the eunuch to take it and explain to me what it meant. He also told the eunuch to urge me to go to the king and beg for mercy for the Jews.

Interviewer: Did you?

Esther: Not at first. When I learned what Mordecai expected me to do, it terrified me. I knew that absolutely no one in their right mind appeared before the king without first being invited. If they did, and the king did not hold out his gold scepter as a sign of approval, that person would die. It had been over a month since the king had last called for me, so I wasn't at all sure that I would be welcomed. So, I sent the eunuch back to Mordecai to explain my situation. I guess I thought that if Mordecai knew that the king hadn't called for me lately, he would understand and would find another way to rescue the Jews.

Interviewer: Did he understand your predicament and what he was asking you to do?

Esther: Yes, he understood. In fact, he actually had a pretty good argument. He reminded me that I was a Jew, and being the queen wasn't enough to save even me. After all, the order had been for the annihilation of all the Jews. Mordecai was convinced God would rescue them somehow—if not through me, then through someone else. Then he suggested that this was the reason I—a Jew—was in the palace in the first place. Perhaps this was God's way of preparing for this day.

Interviewer: Sounds like he laid a pretty heavy guilt trip on you.

Esther: It does sound that way, doesn't it? But I guess deep down I always knew I was in the palace for a reason. I just didn't know what—or when—I would find out. And I certainly didn't expect something that could cost me my life!

Interviewer: What did you do?

Esther: Well, I sent back word that I would go see King Xerxes, and if I died because of it, then so be it. However, before I went, I told Mordecai that my servant girls and I would fast and pray. And I asked Mordecai and others to do the same.

Interviewer: What happened next? I imagine you had to be nearly sick with fear over what you were preparing to do.

Esther: Oh, I was. I fasted and prayed and wracked my brain trying to figure out the best way to go about doing this. It was by far the hardest thing I'd ever been asked to do. Honestly, I wasn't at all sure I was up to the task.

Well, three days later, after first getting my backup plan in motion, I ever so meticulously put on my royal robes. When I was sure I looked the best I possibly could, I slowly walked through the inner court of the palace and up to the king's hall. There I stood, praying like you wouldn't believe that the king would accept me and hold out his gold scepter.

Interviewer: That had to have been terrifying for you. What were you thinking? What happened? Did he welcome you?

Esther: Well, I stood there for what seemed like an eternity. I'm sure it was only a few seconds—a minute at the most. But to me, it seemed forever. My hands were sweaty, my knees felt like they would buckle under me any minute, and my heart was beating so loudly that my head and ears were pounding. I honestly thought I was going to pass out. But just at that moment, I saw the gold scepter lift. I couldn't believe my eyes! He was actually holding out the scepter for me.

Interviewer: Oh, my goodness, you must have been so relieved.

Esther: You better believe it! I took a deep breath, got my bearings, and walked toward the king until I was able to touch the tip of the scepter and bow before him. The king then asked me what I wanted and told me he would give me whatever it was—up to half the kingdom! How I wished that was what I was about to ask for. That would have been so much easier. Anything would have been easier than what I needed to ask. Instead, I had come with a much greater, more life-threatening need. But I chickened out, and instead of asking him to rescind his decree to have the Jews killed, I invited the king to a banquet I would prepare the next day and asked him to bring along Haman, his right-hand man.

Interviewer: So that was the backup plan!

Esther: Well, you see, I still wasn't at all sure I was up to the task. Oh, I wanted to be, but I'm afraid I just needed more time to work up my courage. And as it turned out, I think what I offered as my Plan B was actually God's Plan A.

Interviewer: How so?

Esther: Let me tell you more about that later. Anyway, first let's fast forward to the next day. We're at the banquet, and Xerxes and Haman are eating, drinking, and thoroughly enjoying themselves, when Xerxes asked me what I wanted. It was King Xerxes himself who brought up the subject. Well, that threw me for a loop! I wasn't expecting Xerxes to ask me—I was expected to approach him. Anyway, now there were two sets of eyes just staring at me, wondering, waiting in anticipation to hear what I was after. Well, again, I backed out and instead asked if he and Haman would come to yet another banquet I would prepare for them the next day. I could tell Xerxes was getting very curious, so I promised him that tomorrow I would ask him what it was I really wanted. That seemed to satisfy Xerxes and also gave me a bit more time. Believe me, that night I did some major praying.

Meanwhile, God was at work on two other fronts! Now comes the part where I think I was doing God's Plan A all along. To begin with, after leaving that first banquet, Haman was on cloud nine. He was feeling especially important, and he began bragging about how I had invited only him and the king to a special banquet and how he had another invitation for the very next day. He reminded everyone he ran into about how he had been promoted above all the others in the palace. There seemed to be no end to his gloating. Then, in his typical self-absorbed fashion, he said that everything was meaningless—all the glory and prestige was meaningless as long as Mordecai was at the palace gate, in full view, refusing to bow to him. So Haman's wife and friends suggested that he have gallows built and that the next day Haman should ask the king for permission to have Mordecai hanged. Well, as you can imagine, Haman thought that was a grand idea and instructed his men to get right on it.

Then, the second way God was at work was later that night. The king was having trouble sleeping, so he had an attendant read to him from some historical records. Personally, that would have done the trick for me right then and there! I would have fallen asleep in no time. But the king was still wide awake. So the attendant continued reading and just "happened" to read the part about Mordecai and how he had earlier exposed an assassination plot against the king. King Xerxes asked how Mordecai had been rewarded and learned that nothing had ever been done to repay or honor him for his diligence. This oversight continued to weigh heavy on the king's mind when Haman came knocking at the palace doors the next morning. So the king asked Haman what should be done to show honor to a man the king pleases. Well, Haman thought for sure he was the man the king was referring to, so he presented some really grandiose ideas—royal robe, royal horse with royal emblem on its head, royal parade through town. You get the idea. Imagine Haman's surprise when he found out it wasn't him at all but Mordecai that the king wanted to honor. And not only that, but the king expected Haman himself to carry out the royal treatment of Mordecai!

Interviewer: So much for requesting Mordecai's hanging!

Esther: You got that right! As soon as the grand procession was over, Haman made a beeline for the comforts of home with his tail between his legs and whined to his wife and friends about all that had happened. Well, everyone now saw the writing on the wall— that it was no use for Haman to have ill thoughts about Mordecai now that the king had bestowed such honor on him. But Haman couldn't seem to let it go. Finally his wife and friends just basically told him to get over it and move on.

Interviewer: Did he follow their advice?

Esther: Oh, get this! God's timing is so perfect. Right when Haman was at his lowest, his ride came to pick him up to bring him to my banquet! I'm sure partying with the king was the last thing he felt like doing right then.

Keep in mind that I didn't know that any of these things had happened. I had spent the last few hours preparing the next banquet and readying myself to tell the king what I wanted. Imagine my surprise to see the change in Haman. The day before, he had acted as if he was the life of the party. This time he seemed very subdued and downtrodden. The change in him really puzzled me.

Anyway, shortly into the meal, the king asked what I wanted. I think his curiosity was about to get the best of him. He even reminded me again that whatever it was, he would give it to me—up to half the kingdom! I'm sure he thought that would ease my mind and make it easier for me.

Interviewer: Did it?

Esther: No, not really. Oh, I was flattered that he was making such an effort to reassure me. But he had no clue of the seriousness of what I was about to ask. However, I knew that this time it was now or never. I'm not sure King Xerxes would have accommodated me a third time. So I told him about the situation the Jews were in and begged that he would spare our lives. He asked whose idea it was to destroy them in the first place. When I told him it had been Haman who manipulated the decree, you should have seen the looks on both their faces. Haman turned white as a sheet and cold as ice, whereas Xerxes turned red as blood and hot as fire. Xerxes immediately jumped up to walk off his rage in the palace garden before he said or did anything rash. I guess he remembered that the last time he did something rash, he lost his queen. Meanwhile, Haman began begging me for his life. In despair, Haman, pleading for mercy, fell onto the couch where I was sitting. And it just so happened that this was the exact moment that King Xerxes walked back in. Seeing Haman on the couch with me, and thinking he was assaulting me, made Xerxes even more furious. So he signaled that Haman be killed.

That's the moment when both King Xerxes and I first learned from one of the eunuchs about the gallows Haman had built. Xerxes ordered that Haman be hanged on them just as he had intended for Mordecai.

Interviewer: My goodness, Esther. You were right about all the drama. That was some whirlwind you went through. So, tell me, how does your story end?

Esther: Well, things did calm down a bit. I received all of Haman's property, and Mordecai was given the king's signet ring, which Xerxes had taken away from Haman. I also put Mordecai in charge of my new estate, since I knew absolutely nothing about property management.

Interviewer: And the decree? Were the Jews saved?

Esther: That's a good question! Would you believe I had to approach the king yet again to ask him that? It seems that in all the excitement Xerxes had forgotten my initial request. Anyway, I went before the king again. And again, he received me. And yet again, I asked favor for the Jews. This time King Xerxes had Mordecai write up an order to cancel out Haman's and had Mordecai seal it with the same signet ring that had once been given to Haman. Xerxes made sure that Mordecai understood that this time, whatever was written could not be revoked—ever. I wish you could have seen and heard the celebration as news of the release of their death sentence spread to the Jews throughout Persia. You could not have found a happier race of people anywhere.

Interviewer: Oh, Esther, it has been so wonderful having you in our midst and hearing your story firsthand. Thank you so much for sharing. We have been so blessed to hear how God was at work in your life. Before we let you go, could you give us two or three lessons you learned from your life that we should make an effort to learn?

Esther: It would be my pleasure. First of all, I would say to trust God completely. Most times we are not privileged to see how God has been at work behind the scenes in our lives until the final act is played. I see now that it was God who was causing me to keep putting off asking King Xerxes to spare the lives of the Jews. God needed to lay a little more groundwork to ensure that I would receive a favorable response.

That ties in very closely with the need to go with the flow. Don't try to rush God. And don't try to do everything yourself. Rely on him. Learn to fast and pray. Learn to hear his voice. Allow him to take the lead. Your job is to follow.

Then I would say beware of getting a big head. Haman had finagled his way up to the position as King Xerxes' right-hand man. But he knew nothing about how to handle the honor or position bestowed on him. He began to think himself invincible and better than anyone else—especially the Jews. When God looks at us, he doesn't see positions or knowledge or even beauty. He sees hearts. Instead of having a big head, strive to have a big heart.

Interviewer: Esther, thank you for joining us and blessing us with your story. You led an extraordinary life, and we have been so blessed to meet you. Thank you so much.

DISCUSSION QUESTIONS:

1. Early on, Esther requested that her title as "Queen" be dropped. She pointed out that she was just Esther, a woman much like us. What kind of feelings and emotions did you notice as we heard her tell her story? Was she right in that we modern women run the same gamut of emotions she did?

2. Congratulations! You've just won a year's worth of pampering at Healthy Spa Beauty Ranch in Timbuktu. Visitors, phone calls, and mail are not allowed, so you can spend the whole time totally relaxed, mentally as well as physically. Do you accept the prize? Why or why not?

3. In the space of what appears to be only a few short years, Esther recounts at least three whirlwind experiences she went through—being taken to the palace and placed in a harem, being chosen as the next queen a year later and all the celebration that ensued, and witnessing firsthand the uproar at her second banquet when Haman's plans—past, present, and future—came to light. What whirlwinds have you experienced in your life?

4. When King Xerxes learned about Haman's actions, he became so infuriated that he had to walk away from the situation for a while. Have you ever had to walk away from a situation before you dared open your mouth? Any examples you would be willing to share?

5. It took Esther three tries—and two banquets—before she was able to work up the courage to ask King Xerxes

what she really wanted. And even then, she didn't get an answer, so had to ask yet again. Have you ever had to go through something similar? Perhaps with your parents, husband, boss, or someone else?

6. As Christians, we know that God can work all things out for good. What has happened in your life that you can look back on now and see how God was orchestrating the whole thing all along—people, timing, results, and so forth?

Mary (mother of Jesus, part 1)

Background Reading: Matthew 1:18–2:23; Luke
   1:26-56; 2:1-52
In-Class Reading: Luke 1:26-41; Matthew 1:19-
   25; Luke 2:1-19
Key Verse: Luke 2:19

Interviewer: Welcome, Mary. It is so good to finally have
   you visit with us. We have all been so eager to meet
   you and hear your story. When I first began sched-
   uling these interviews and asked women who they
   most wanted to meet from Bible times, you were by
   far the number one choice.

Mary: Why, thank you so much for those kind words.
   And I must say, I feel privileged to be here as well.

Interviewer: Mary, if you don't mind, since our time
   is so short, let's just jump right in. OK? We have so
   many questions for you that it's hard to know where
   to begin. So let's start with some of the basics. What
   was life like for you growing up? How did you and
   Joseph meet? What was Jesus like as a child? I guess
   we're curious, most of all, to learn how you handled
   all the ups and downs in your life.

Mary: Well, I certainly did have a lot of those! Early on, I would say I was your average Jewish girl. I had the same expectations in life as all my girlfriends—to grow up, get married, and have children. We used to spend hours giggling at the prospect. And although we were discouraged from doing so, we would occasionally check out the boys. Mom would have a fit if she knew I told you that!

Anyway, one day I spied Joseph. Oh, I thought he was about the most handsome boy around. And as I watched him from a distance I saw that he was a hard worker, too. I knew he would be a good provider. But there was one problem—Joseph was about as shy and quiet as I was. I thought he would never notice me and once he did, I thought he'd never work up the courage to talk to me! You know, it got to be kind of exhausting, but I chased after him until he caught me.

Interviewer: My goodness, Mary. Whatever do you mean by that?

Mary: Well, every chance I could, I would walk past the carpenter shop where he worked. More times than not, it was really pretty far out of my way, but I didn't mind. I just wanted to see him—and hopefully, for him to notice me. At first, all he seemed to do was give me quick glances every so often. And then, maybe it was wishful thinking on my part, but it seemed that his quick glances seemed to be getting a little longer. I thought he would never make the effort to talk to me! But finally, he did. And we learned that, just as I suspected all along, we were meant for each other. Before too long, we were engaged and you couldn't have found a happier girl in all of Nazareth.

Interviewer: Tell us about your engagement. What was that like?

Mary: Well, it really was pretty low-key—except for maybe my squeals of delight occasionally. We were both too poor to have a huge party to celebrate. We just celebrated with our families and closest friends. But that was OK. Neither of us was very outgoing, and we were never really comfortable being the center of attention anyway! We were much happier staying in the background where eyes weren't focused on us.

In the beginning, our engagement period was pretty much like everyone else's. Joseph began building a house for us, and I began to pay close attention as Mom taught me about caring for a husband, family, and home. I was so full of expectations and dreams. That is, until Gabriel showed up. Once he showed up, my life—our life—was never the same.

Interviewer: Who was Gabriel? Perhaps another young man vying for your attention?

Mary: Oh, no, nothing like that! Although, I must admit, he did get my attention! Gabriel was an angel who appeared to me one day out of nowhere. Actually, he nearly scared the wits out of me! I was deep in thought about Joseph when Gabriel popped in, unannounced I might add, and started talking. But it wasn't like normal talk. He was so excited about what he was saying that it almost sounded as if he was yelling it to the whole world, although there was no one else around. It was just him and me. I can still hear his first words: "Greetings, favored woman! The Lord is with you!" He was announcing it as if I'd won a prize of some sort! And he called me "woman." That really caught me by surprise. Yes, I was engaged and certainly old enough, but it was the first time I'd heard that said about me out loud. Woman. To think, I was a woman and hadn't even realized it! When did that happen? I didn't feel any different!

Anyway, I was a bit confused and scared. Who was this guy, and what did he mean when he said, "The Lord is with you"? My expression must have spoken volumes to him, because he went on to tell me to not be afraid—that I was going to be blessed with a son. While my fear may have lessened, my confusion increased. What in the world was he talking about? I wasn't even married yet! How could I possibly get pregnant before then? Surely he must have the wrong girl—I mean, "woman." Besides, I was young and from a poor family. How could I possibly be the chosen one?

But he kept insisting—even going so far as to tell me that my cousin Elizabeth was going to have a baby as well! Now I was in outright shock! Elizabeth was old—I mean, really old! She was way too old to be having a baby. Then, as if to seal the deal, Gabriel said, "For nothing is impossible with God." My head was spinning so fast. I'm not sure how the angel understood my stammering, but I said something about being the Lord's servant and being willing to do whatever he wanted me to do. Then, just as quickly as he came, Gabriel left. And there I stood with my confusion, fear, shock, and now, lots and lots of questions.

Interviewer: What in the world did you do once the shock wore off?

Mary: Well, I could tell I was different somehow. And I knew I had to tell Joseph right away what had happened. I thought maybe he could help me sort it all out. But he was just as confused and upset as I was. Then it dawned on me—what if he no longer wanted to marry me? How was I going to handle the public disgrace of being pregnant outside of marriage, as well as a broken engagement? What if Joseph decided to divorce me? Or worse yet, have me stoned? It was almost more than I could take. So I ran home to talk with Mom. She would understand and know what to do—or so I thought.

Interviewer: I gather that she was just as clueless as to what to do as the two of you were.

Mary: Right. She didn't know what to do either. My life seemed to be spinning out of control, and I had no idea how to stop it. The next few days were a blur. How everyone in town found out about what was going on, I'll never know. I know Joseph and Mom wouldn't have spoken publicly about such things— at least not yet. It was too soon. After all, that would have brought embarrassment to the family. When your family's facing a "scandal" such as this, the last thing you do is rush right out and tell the whole world! But it was obvious from the stares and finger-pointing that everyone knew I had somehow done something terribly wrong.

Interviewer: Mary, I can't imagine how you must have felt. That had to have been so hard for you. I think I would have been tempted to run away.

Mary: Well, it's funny that you said that, because that's sort of what I did. A few days later, I headed for the hills—to Judea, that is—to visit Elizabeth and her husband, Zechariah. I actually didn't know where else to go. And ever since Gabriel had told me about Elizabeth having a baby, I couldn't seem to get her out of my mind.

Interviewer: Did Elizabeth and Zechariah know about what was going on with you—your pregnancy and public humiliation?

Mary: Not at first. But it didn't take long! The minute I greeted Elizabeth, she said the baby within her literally jumped for joy, and she was filled with the Holy Spirit. Then she told me that my child was blessed and that she felt honored that the mother of her Lord would visit her.

Interviewer: What did you think when Elizabeth said all these things? And what did Zechariah have to say about all this?

Mary: Well, Elizabeth's greeting did give me a small measure of comfort and reassurance, even though everything seemed to be so difficult at the moment. It was actually Elizabeth's greeting that caused me to realize what God was asking of me. I felt so honored and humbled that I would be the chosen one to bring the long-awaited, promised Savior into the world.

As for Zechariah, he didn't say a word! But that's a whole other story! The short version is that when God told him that Elizabeth would have a baby, he didn't believe him and pointed out all the reasons why she couldn't. So, he was stricken dumb and was not able to utter even a sound until after Elizabeth's baby was born.

Interviewer: Well, now, aren't you glad you didn't argue with Gabriel—and God?

Mary: I most certainly was! Can you imagine not being able to talk on top of everything else? That would have made things even that much harder.

Interviewer: So, how long did you stay with Elizabeth? And did you have any idea what was going on at home while you were gone?

Mary: I actually stayed about three months—long enough to get over the morning sickness and come to terms with what I had been chosen to do.

Meanwhile, Joseph was coming to terms with everything himself. I learned later that at one time he had decided he would break our engagement. He had planned to do it quietly and with dignity so I wouldn't be disgraced any more than I already was. But just as he was thinking all this through, an angel appeared to him in a dream, reassuring him that this was meant to be—that this was God's will and that I had done nothing wrong. The angel told him to go ahead and marry me and to name the baby "Jesus." So, that's when Joseph came after me and brought me home to be his wife.

Interviewer: That had to have been such a huge relief for you—not only because Joseph was obedient to God, but also because you could finally settle down and begin to move on with your life.

Mary: Yes, but I soon learned that settling down was not in my near future, and my traveling days far from over.

Interviewer: What do you mean?

Mary: Well, a few weeks later we learned about a census Joseph was required to participate in. So, since Joseph's family was originally from Bethlehem in Judea, we had to travel back to Judea to register. That was no small distance from Nazareth—especially when you're pregnant! And it seemed even longer to me since I had just come from there, visiting Elizabeth.

Not too long into the journey, I began to notice that I didn't quite feel right. I couldn't put my finger on it, but by the time we actually got into town, I was beginning to feel pretty miserable. We went from place to place, trying to find a room to rent. Finally I told Joseph that we had to stop—that I could not go any farther. So with the next innkeeper he made arrangements for us to spend the night in his stables with the animals. It wasn't glamorous by any stretch of the imagination, and the smell was almost more than I could stomach. But it was the only thing available. I was so thankful to finally have a place to lie down, stretch out, and get some rest. But no matter what I did, I couldn't seem to get comfortable. It wasn't too long until I began to experience pain.

They were different from any I'd ever had before, and they seemed to be getting worse and worse and more and more frequent. I finally realized the baby was coming, and that terrified me! I had always pictured me giving birth in my own home with Mom at my side, holding my hand and comforting me—telling me everything would be all right. It wasn't supposed to happen like this! But this was it. At times, I didn't see how I could ever make it through. I was in so much misery and pain; I really thought I might die. But Joseph was so good. He kept reminding me how special this baby was—that he was more special than any baby that had ever been born—or would ever be born! He was right, of course. This baby—God's baby—God's own Son—was about to be born. And I was the one woman in all of history to be chosen for the task. Then I thought, "Why would God have chosen me if he didn't think I was up to it?" And all of a sudden, the time, place, smell, noise, and pain didn't matter at all. The only thing that mattered was this tiny baby God had entrusted to Joseph and me.

Then, before I knew it, there he was—all ten fingers and ten toes, and as wrinkled as any baby I'd ever seen! But oh, was he beautiful! He took my breath away. It was then that I realized that I may have given him life today, but someday he would be giving me something so much more. He was the promised one who would give me eternal life.

Interviewer: Wow. Mary, you have me almost speechless. I can just picture the three of you now—all huddled together, with the straw and animals circled around you. That family portrait of yours is the first one we show our babies. And it's the very one we re-enact every Christmas.

So, what happened next? I'm assuming that in all the excitement Joseph did remember to register for the census!

Mary: You know, the next morning when he walked out of the stables to take care of that, I'm pretty sure he was walking a bit taller and prouder. And I thought he was handsome before! I had such admiration for him.

Interviewer: Mary, what did you and baby Jesus do while Joseph was gone and it was just the two of you?

Mary: We did a lot of bonding. I nursed him and held him the entire time. I didn't want to put him down—not even for a second. I talked and sang to him. I wanted him to hear my voice, to feel my presence, to know that everything was OK—that I would always be there for him. I tell myself I did it all for Jesus. But if I were to be completely honest, I think I did it more for me. I knew this baby was destined for something big and that time would pass way too quickly. I knew that someday I might not be able to hold him, hug him, or talk to him as mothers do. It was almost as if I was making up for lost time ahead of time. Does that make any sense?

Anyway, when Joseph got back, he insisted I let go so I could get some much-needed rest. But that was so very hard. It just tore my heart that I had to let him go so soon. It just didn't seem right. It was almost as if I had a premonition of the agony of what was to come. But I knew Joseph was right. So I left Jesus in his capable hands while I got some rest. And it's a good thing I did, too! It wasn't long before we had some very unexpected company!

Interviewer: My goodness, Mary. What kind of company would pop in on you at a time like this? And how did they find you all tucked away in a stable among the animals?

Mary: That's a good question—and one I wondered about myself. Actually, some shepherds had rushed into the village of Bethlehem purposely to find us, telling everyone they met along the way about what had happened to them. It seems an angel came to visit them out in the fields the night Jesus was born and told them about his birth—even down to the exact place to find him and what he would be wearing! The shepherds were so excited and amazed to see Jesus. It just reinforced to Joseph and me what an absolutely marvelous one-of-a-kind baby and experience this was. It naturally made me wonder about what was ahead. While Joseph thanked the shepherds for coming, I sat back and took in the scene, treasuring the moment and pondering the future. I somehow knew there would be some interesting, and probably painful, days ahead for all of us! And boy, was I ever right!

Interviewer: Sounds like you were still riding the roller coaster of ups and downs. How long did the shepherds stay, and what happened once they left?

Mary: Oh, they didn't stay very long at all because they had to get back to their flocks. Then, eight days later, we took the baby to be circumcised. That was also when Joseph officially gave him the name Jesus, just as the angel had told each of us to do. Then we headed to Jerusalem to dedicate Jesus and to present him to the Lord God. After that, rather than travel the 70 or so miles back to Nazareth, we decided to stay in nearby Bethlehem for a time. I think both Joseph and I were ready for life to settle down for us so we could start living as normal families did. But if there's one thing I quickly learned about being the mother of the

Son of God, it's that nothing was ever normal—at least not for very long periods of time!

Interviewer: What do you mean by that?

Mary: We had been in Bethlehem only a couple of years when some wise men came knocking at our door. When they saw Jesus, they immediately bowed down and worshipped him. Then they gave him all kinds of gifts—gold, incense, myrrh. It was all so unusual. Joseph asked them how it was they had come to find Jesus. Then they told us this amazing story about seeing his star and following it first to Jerusalem and then on to Bethlehem. It was really all quite amazing. To think—our son had his very own special star! God never ceased to amaze us. Then, when they left, we noticed that these wise men didn't head back the same direction they had come. That puzzled us, but we figured if they had traveled hundreds of miles to find this tiny baby in the first place, then they would have no trouble finding their way back home. After all, they were wise men. But it seemed to us as if they were taking the long way home!

Anyway, I think it was the very night after their visit that Joseph had another dream in which an angel spoke to him. This time the angel told Joseph to flee to Egypt because Herod, the king, was trying to find Jesus in order to kill him. Well, we wasted no time! Actually, we didn't even wait for daylight! As soon as Joseph woke up from the dream, we packed up and left! That was such a long, hard trip. Joseph wanted to get as many miles between us and Bethlehem as he could, so we traveled as hard and fast as possible, considering we had a toddler in tow. The 100-plus miles to Egypt were so hard on us, but God was faithful and kept us safe. We learned later that Herod had had all the boys 2 years old and younger killed—all because he felt threatened by Jesus. My, how that broke my heart. I cried so many tears those next few days—not just tears of sorrow for the mothers who had lost their sons but also tears of joy for our safety. I was so thankful for Joseph's quick and ready obedience to whatever God told him to do.

Interviewer: How long did you stay in Egypt, and what did you think of it? Did you like it there?

Mary: I didn't like Egypt at all. Actually, none of us did. But we knew we had been sent there by God for our own protection, so we stuck it out. We stayed there until Herod died. But even then we didn't rush back home. Oh, I wanted to, believe me! But Joseph insisted we wait until God told us it was time. Finally, one morning Joseph told me the Lord had appeared to him in another dream and told him it was safe to head back to Israel. So we started out, all the while trying to decide where in Israel to move back to. We had grown up in Nazareth in Galilee, and we still had family there. We had always hoped someday to go back home. But then, Bethlehem in Judea was closer, and it was where Jesus had been born and where we had lived a couple of years before going to Egypt. We still had a lot of friends living there. I guess we would have been happy with either place.

Our main concern was to go where God wanted us to go. As we traveled, we prayed for direction from God. Finally, a few days outside Bethlehem, Joseph had yet another dream in which the Lord told him to go the extra distance and return to Nazareth. I was so excited to be headed home! My heart began racing at just the thought of it. Home. That one word never sounded so good!

Interviewer: Was it as wonderful as you expected?

Mary: Oh, it was. I wanted so badly to get settled in a permanent home of our own and start living a normal life. And once we were in a routine again, I began to feel as if we were finally living the life I'd always dreamed. Joseph set up shop again, working as a carpenter, and I set out to get our home in order. All was going so well. We were so happy. But every time I began to get even the least bit complacent and comfortable in my role as wife and mother, something would happen that would cause me to stop and realize all over again that my firstborn, Jesus, was not your typical child. In my heart, I always knew it and never forgot it. It's just that sometimes things would happen that would cause me to have no choice but to step back to pause and ponder.

Interviewer: Like what kind of things? Anything specific you could share with us?

Mary: Not really. Although there was this one time that stands out. Jesus was probably about 12 at the time, and we had gone to Jerusalem.

Interviewer: Mary, I really hate to interrupt, but I just realized what time it is. I suspect we're not going to have enough time to do this story justice. Tell you what, rather than hurry through it, I'm wondering if it would be possible for you to come back and finish telling us your life's story. Do you think you could work us into your schedule again in the next week or two?

Mary: Sure. I would be glad to do that. And you're right. That is another long story. And I have many other things I'd really like to share with all of you as well. I'd be delighted to come back.

Interviewer: Thank you so much, Mary. Let's go ahead and wind up this first part of your interview, and then the two of us can look at our calendars and see when the best time for you to visit us again might be. OK?

Mary: Sounds good to me.

Interviewer: Mary, we have been curious to learn from the women of Bible times the most important lessons they learned from their lives. Do you have two or three that come to mind that you could share with us that would help us grow in our walk with the Lord?

Mary: Oh, of course. Let me think for just a minute. Well, even though my situation was a bit different, I would say one thing would be to always be alert to how God wants to use you. It doesn't matter if you're rich or poor, young or old, smart or not so smart. He has something he needs you to do. Always be willing to at least try what you feel he's leading you toward. You might be surprised at the success you'll have when he's the instigator. And when you are successful, be sure to give God the credit he deserves. There is no way I could have handled being the mother of Jesus without God's help and support every step of the way. I'm still not sure why he chose me, but I like to think it was because I was humble enough to realize how much help I would need and that through the tough times as well as the good times he could rely on me to rely on him. Remember, your life may not turn out exactly as you dreamed or expected. But with God in control, it will turn out far better than you could ever imagine.

You know, God doesn't always choose to use the most talented or gifted but instead uses those who are most willing to be used by him. This means being obedient to whatever he says or asks. I was always so proud of Joseph. Every time he had a dream with a message from the Lord, he didn't argue or complain or spend days deciding whether or not to do what he was told. He always obeyed immediately. He was a perfect example to our children—and to me, for that matter—of what it meant to be obedient to God.

Interviewer: Mary, thank you for joining us and blessing us with your story. You were truly a remarkable woman, and we have been so blessed to meet you. Thank you so much for taking time to be with us. And thank you for agreeing to come back again.

DISCUSSION QUESTIONS:

1. Early on, Mary reminisces about the first time she heard herself referred to as a woman. There are probably many of us who found ourselves taken aback the first time we realized we had crossed from girlhood to womanhood. Do you remember the first time you were referred to as a woman? If so, would you share that experience?

2. Although Mary was willing to be used by God, Gabriel's announcement to Mary sent her life into a bit of a tailspin. Mary talks about how she didn't know what to do or how to gain control. Ultimately, she retreated for a few weeks, sought counsel from Elizabeth, and refocused on this sudden turn of events in her life. Have you ever been through a time when you felt as if your life was running out of control, and you were clueless as to what to do about it? What did you do to regain some measure of control?

3. As in the case of Mary, we've read many accounts in the Bible where an angel has shown up unexpectedly to pass on a message from God. Other times, as in Joseph's case, messages came in the form of dreams. How do you think God determined which method to use when? And how does he give us messages today?

4. Mary talks about the unusual circumstances of Jesus' birth and how it was nothing like she had planned. If you are a mother, were there any unusual circumstances surrounding the birth of your child or children?

5. Many women can understand Mary's dream of settling down with a home, husband, and children. Yet, for years, she and Joseph found themselves moving from place to place before they were finally led back home to Nazareth. Mary said the word "home" never sounded so good. What does the word "home" mean to you?

6. Obedience. We've talked about this before and most likely will again. What did obedience to God mean to Mary? To Joseph?

Mary (mother of Jesus, part 2)

Background Reading: Luke 2:41-52; John 2:1-
11; John 19:25-27; John 20
In-Class Reading: Luke 2:41-52; John 2:1-11
Key Verse: Luke 2:51b

Interviewer: Thank you, Mary, for visiting with us once again. We enjoyed so much your first visit and hearing your stories about the angel's appearance to you, Jesus' birth, and your early travels. I hope we didn't inconvenience you too much by asking you to come back and tell us more.

Mary: Of course not! I loved visiting with all of you as well and have looked forward to my return trip.

Interviewer: Mary, when we last talked, you were saying that there were times in Jesus' life that caused you to pause and ponder. You were just beginning to tell us a story about Jesus when he was around 12. Do you remember what you were going to share with us?

Mary: Yes, I sure do. After all, when you lose your child for three days, you don't quickly forget it!

Interviewer: Jesus was lost for three days! You know, most of us can identify with the feeling of losing a child temporarily, maybe a few minutes, but not for days! What happened?

Mary: Well, we had gone to Jerusalem for the Feast of the Passover—"we" being all of our family and some close friends who were traveling with us in a caravan. Not only was it safer to travel in a large group, it was a lot more fun as well. Anyway, after the Passover, our caravan began to head back home to Nazareth. We had traveled the better part of the day before I realized Jesus was missing. I thought Jesus was with Joseph, and Joseph thought Jesus was with me.

Interviewer: But I thought you said you were all traveling together.

Mary: We were, sort of. It was customary for the women and younger children to be at the head of the caravan and the men and older boys to bring up the rear. Jesus, being 12, could easily have been included in either group. So, that's how Joseph and I came to be split up, and that's why we missed the fact that Jesus wasn't with us. When I realized what had happened, I felt so awful! What kind of a mother was I to lose one of her own children? You must think I'm terrible!

Interviewer: Oh, Mary, not at all. In fact, something similar happens even today. Many times families end up going to church in two separate vehicles, and when they leave, unless they're careful, a child could be left behind. So, don't feel bad; it's an easy thing to do—especially if you have more than one child to watch out for. What did you do when you first realized Jesus wasn't with either one of you?

Mary: Well, I was never one to panic first. After all, we were traveling in a rather large caravan of family and friends, and Jesus did have a lot of childhood buddies. I thought perhaps he was with some of them. So we began asking around to see if maybe one of them had seen him. But after searching and looking everywhere and asking all of his friends, we still had not found him. It finally became obvious he had been left behind in Jerusalem. We had no choice but to head back to where we had last seen him. And believe me, finding him was not easy!

Interviewer: Did the entire caravan turn around and go with you back to Jerusalem to search for Jesus?

Mary: No, we couldn't expect everyone to turn around because of our child. Joseph and I and the rest of our children went back on our own. Oh, Joseph and I were not happy with him. Remember, Jesus was 12! He was old enough to know better and should have had no problem staying with us and being where he was expected to be. But as we learned later, that was exactly the problem.

Interviewer: What was the problem?

Mary: Well, when we first got back to Jerusalem, we searched the city high and low, top to bottom, inside and out, in search of Jesus. He wasn't anywhere we thought he might be. And when we finally found him, he was in the Temple, of all places! The first thing we did was question him: "Where have you been?"

"Didn't you notice the caravan leaving?" "How long have you been in the Temple?" "Why are you even in the Temple in the first place?" "Do you have any idea how long we've been looking for you?"

Interviewer: What kind of answers did you get? What was Jesus' excuse?

Mary: He turned to us so matter of factly and said, "Why did you have to look so hard for me? Didn't you realize I had to be in my Father's house?"

Interviewer: How did you respond to that?

Mary: Well, initially I just stood there with my mouth hanging open, trying to process it all. You see, the problem was that Jesus was exactly where his heavenly Father expected him to be, which took precedence over where his earthly father (and mother) expected him to be. But at the time, Joseph and I didn't fully understand what he said to us. You know, the older Jesus got, that seemed to happen more and more often. But anyway, we made him leave the Temple to go back to Nazareth with us, which he willingly did. Jesus was always obedient and respectful toward us.

Anyway, as the days and weeks passed, I couldn't seem to get the scene or his words that day out of my mind. I kept replaying everything over and over. That experience was a turning point for me. It was then that I began to realize that Jesus was no longer the baby or the young boy I had been given to bring up. He was now turning into the man God expected him to be. Over the years, Jesus had grown from a typical baby to a normal toddler and then a young boy with bumps, bruises, and scrapes all along the way—just like any other child. He went to school and learned his lessons like all the other boys his age, and Joseph taught him the basics of carpentry—how to hammer nails and saw pieces of wood. It gave me both pride and anguish to realize that before long I was going to have to let him go. I worried about him so much.

Interviewer: Oh, I think many of us in this room can identify with that feeling very well. I think the anxiety of letting your child go is universal. After all, once we become a mother, we are a mother for the rest of our lives, no matter how old our child gets! And once they leave, you are no longer there to guide their decisions or smooth over their hurts.

Mary, could you share with us some more stories about Jesus? What are some of your favorite memories?

Mary: Oh, my, I have so many. It's hard to know where to begin. I would definitely have to say that one of my favorite memories would be the first miracle I saw him perform. By then Jesus had been teaching and preaching and had a following of men he called his disciples who traveled with him. Anyway, all of us—myself, Jesus, and his disciples—happened to be at the wedding feast of a dear friend of ours in Cana in Galilee. During the course of the celebration, I noticed that our host was quickly running out of wine, which was a real social blunder in our day. I merely pointed out that fact to Jesus and told him how sorry I felt for our host. After all, I could just imagine his embarrassment when everyone at the party realized there was no more wine. That wasn't anything I'd wish on my worst enemy. To run out of wine was almost unheard of!

I guess I was thinking that perhaps Jesus and a couple of his disciples would secretly slip out and get some more for the festivities. But what he said to me instead was, "My time has not yet come." Whatever did that mean? You know, it seemed that he was always saying things I found hard to understand. But at the time, even though his words sounded harsh, as if he didn't plan to do a thing about it, his eyes told me something very different. I told the servants to do whatever Jesus told them to do. Long story short, he had the servants fill six large jars full of water and had them pour some into a glass and take it directly to the master of the banquet. Imagine our surprise to learn that what was water just seconds before was now wine—and good wine, at that! I wasn't sure what I had been expecting, but it certainly wasn't that! Up until that time, Jesus hadn't performed any miracles, so it wasn't something I even dreamed he could do!

Once again, I was left speechless. I stood there in awe of him, wondering what the future held for my precious son.

Interviewer: Since you said this was his first miracle, I'm assuming there were others as well?

Mary: Oh, my, yes. Most of them I only heard about. But over the next few years, there were a lot of them. Jesus had such a heart for the children and the less fortunate. And it seemed he was always healing someone—the blind, the deaf, the crippled, the sick, the leprous—even raising the dead. Wherever there was a need, Jesus was often there, ready to come to their aid. Usually all they had to do was trust him and do what he said.

And he always made sure people were taken care of. While he could go for days without eating, he realized others couldn't, so he was always feeding the hungry. On at least two occasions, he fed thousands with only a handful of fish and bread.

He walked on water, too. And he stopped storms in mid air. And it seemed he could turn old fishing nets into powerful magnets, attracting fish by the hundreds. It seemed there was nothing he couldn't do, which is why I had trouble understanding how he could allow some people to dislike him so much — actually hate him. After all, it seemed to me that if he could heal people and raise them from the dead, and cast out demons and evil spirits, surely he could take away the evil that some people held in their heart towards him. With each taunting or degrading remark I heard, I was more deeply crushed. In retrospect, that may be the reason why I wasn't as involved in his adult life as much as other mothers were in their sons' lives. I think he knew how much it pained me to see him ridiculed. I think it was his way of sparing me as much pain and suffering as he could. Does that make sense?

Interviewer: More than you realize. Any mother here can understand the pain and anguish she would feel if her child was mistreated. Our natural instinct is to jump to their defense and rescue them and take away their hurts. Yet, as they approach and reach adulthood, while the feelings of protection remain, our ability to jump in and rescue them diminishes considerably. As Christians, you have to let them live their lives and trust them to stay true to the values you instilled in them and pray that they follow God's leading. When bad things happen, sometimes all you can do is sit back and trust God. You need to trust that he knows what he's doing in the life of your child.

Mary, I realize we may be dragging up painful memories, but how did you handle the terrible events leading up to Jesus' death?

Mary: You know, the days and weeks leading up to his death had been especially hard for me. I knew that something was about to happen, and I knew it would be awful. I didn't know what, but I could see it in my son's eyes. When our eyes met, I saw not only longing but also fear, anguish, sadness, and sorrow.

Then, when things began to happen, it was as if my mind could no longer think at all. Instead, it was all feelings—one after another. When he was arrested, I felt the chains around my own wrists and legs. When he was beaten, I felt the sting of the whip on my own back. When he fell under the weight of the cross, my own knees buckled under the weight of grief. When the nails were hammered into his hands and feet, I felt every pounding strike of the hammer. And as his heart was breaking, I felt my own breaking as well.

As Jesus was hanging on the cross, our eyes met once again. It was then I felt love like I had never known. Oh, I knew Jesus loved me—and had since the day he was born. But this time was different. This time the look of love was so intense that I felt as if my heart would explode and jump out of my chest. This was a love that seemed to say, "You're special. I'm doing this for you."

Interviewer: Wow. Mary, it's hard to know what to say. What happened next? How does your story end?

Mary: Well, just before he died, Jesus entrusted me into the care of John, one of his disciples. And it was with John that I lived out the rest of my days.

Interviewer: Why didn't Jesus ask your other children to care for you in your old age? And didn't it seem strange, considering everything else going on and the pain he was obviously in, that he would be so concerned about your care?

Mary: Well, Jesus was my oldest. And since Joseph's death, my protector. In my day, it was the responsibility of the oldest son to care for his parents. So I'm sure Jesus felt an obligation to make sure I would be looked after.

Interviewer: Why didn't he just have his oldest brother take over the responsibility?

Mary: That's really hard to say. It's speculation, but here's what I think. John was a favorite disciple of Jesus. And at a time when most people didn't understand Jesus, John did. John trusted him. John stood by him. It was John who was standing by me throughout the whole ordeal of Jesus' crucifixion, helping me, and making sure I was OK.

Jesus' brothers and sisters weren't the ones standing next to me. At the time, they had come to resent and mistrust Jesus and sometimes acted as if they were even embarrassed to have him as a brother. They didn't understand. Later, some did. But at the time, they were so confused. I think Jesus wanted me in the home of someone who had loved him as much as I had—a home where I wouldn't be subjected to more ridicule or more negative talk about him. And maybe, just maybe, Jesus wanted me with John so I could be one of the first ones to hear about his Resurrection from the dead.

Interviewer: How would your being with John have made a difference in that regard?

Mary: Well, it was John, along with Peter, who went darting off to the tomb the morning Mary Magdalene discovered that the tomb was empty—that Jesus' body had disappeared. When he came back and told me, I could hardly believe what I was hearing. I was so excited. Some feared his body had been stolen, but I somehow knew that something bigger—something more wonderful—was happening. And sure enough, it was.

Mary Magdalene was actually the first one to see Jesus alive again and talk with him. Then others got to as well, including Peter and John and the other disciples. Then he appeared to and talked to his brother James. When James came and told me how he finally understood and was a believer, I could not have been happier.

Interviewer: Mary, I haven't found anywhere in the Scriptures that say whether or not you got to talk to Jesus after his Resurrection. Did you?

Mary: I did. But I doubt that the Scriptures would, or could, record such a moment. You see, I got to visit with Jesus alone—just the two of us. We cried. We laughed. We hugged. We cried some more. I touched his scars. I asked him why. He said it was for me. He had to die for me. And not just for me, but for every other human being. We cried even more. He wiped my tears. I looked into his eyes again, and this time I didn't see an unspoken message or a longing. I only saw love—the same look of love I had seen in those last moments on the cross. A love that was so pure, so deep, and so personal that it is indescribable. A love straight from the heart. And I'm convinced, a love that will always remain no matter what people do. While a tear may trickle down his cheek every time we disappoint him, his love for us will always remain. It's almost as if the same nails that secured him to the cross also secured his love for us.

Interviewer: His love. Mary, that seems like the perfect place to bring our interview to a close. But before we let you go, I realize you've done this before, but I wonder if you have another life lesson we should learn.

Mary: Not really. My only suggestion is that you take the time and make the effort to look into Jesus' eyes for yourself. Really look. If you'll do that, I am certain you'll see what I see—love—compassionate, forgiving, unquestionable love.

Interviewer: Thank you, Mary, for joining us again and sharing your story. You are truly an amazing woman, and we have been blessed beyond measure to get to know you.

DISCUSSION QUESTIONS:

1. After finding Jesus in the Temple in Jerusalem, Mary said that Jesus was exactly where his heavenly Father expected him to be, which took precedence over where his earthly father (and mother) expected him to be. We often hear missionaries say that some of their own family members, especially parents, didn't understand why they would choose to go to a foreign field. Can anyone share a personal experience of just such a feeling?

2. If ever there was a mother entitled to bragging rights, it was Mary. Instead of doing so, she "paused and pondered" or was "speechless and in awe." When was the last time you swelled with pride because of something a family member or close friend did—something that caused you to pause and ponder or left you speechless and in awe?

3. Mary challenges us to look into Jesus' eyes. How do we do that?

4. If you've ever lost a child, then you can identify with the emotions Mary felt—or can you? Knowing she had lost the Son of God, do you think her emotions were more pronounced than ours at a time like that, or do you think they would be about the same?

5. Mary talks about how painful it was to see and hear her son ridiculed and mistreated, and wondered why Jesus didn't perform a miracle that would make everyone like him. Why do you think Jesus didn't do that?

6. Mary speculated as to why Jesus put John in charge of her. Why do you think Jesus opted for John rather than a family member?

Rhoda

Background Reading: Acts 12:1-19
In-Class Reading: Acts 12:1-19
Key Verses: Acts 12:13-15

Interviewer: Good morning, Rhoda. It is so good of you to join us and share your story with us. We have been talking to women of Bible times, learning not only about them but also about their relationship with God. Rhoda, I'm sorry to have to say this, but a lot of us don't know a whole lot about you. Would you mind sharing your life's story with us? You seem so young to be immortalized in the pages of Bible history—to be so famous.

Rhoda: Immortalized? Famous? I never thought of myself that way! There's not much to tell about me or my life. I always felt so insecure—so different from other girls my age. As you may know, since my family was very poor, I became a servant girl at a very young age. That's really the only kind of life I ever knew.

Interviewer: I imagine that had to have been rough for you, working so hard instead of enjoying childhood like the other girls.

Rhoda: Oh, it was hard—but probably not as much as you might think. You see, I was excited at first to be hired on as a servant. Yes, the days were long and the work was hard, but the extra money helped my family so much. And I was glad to be able to help.

Interviewer: Rhoda, what kinds of things were you expected to do as a servant?

Rhoda: I didn't do anything out of the ordinary. I did the normal stuff people have come to associate with servants. I basically did what I was told. I did a lot of sweeping and dusting, believe me! I also scrubbed clothes and washed dishes. And very often, I helped in the kitchen. But my favorite job of all was the door.

Interviewer: The door? What do you mean by that?

Rhoda: Well, anytime a visitor came to the house and knocked on the door, I was the one in charge of opening it, seeing who it was, and reporting to Ms. Mary. It was always so exciting when I heard a knock. Since Ms. Mary had a lot of friends, it could be any number of people. But most of the time, it turned out to be one of her Christian friends. At first I wasn't too sure of them. But they always treated me so kindly and were so polite, that I soon began to look forward to their visits. These Christians always seemed to brighten my day—and Ms. Mary's as well.

Interviewer: Could you tell us about Ms. Mary? What was she like?

Rhoda: She was an outstanding Christian woman and one of the nicest people you could ever meet. One of her sons, John Mark, became pretty famous later on when he traveled some with Paul and Barnabas on their missionary journeys. Anyway, he was quite a handsome young man—and one on whom I had a serious crush for a while. That was back when I was a bit more naïve. I came to learn that guys like John Mark didn't have much to do with servant girls. Oh, he was kind enough to me and always spoke to me. It's just that it wasn't the proper thing to do— getting too friendly with the hired help. Besides, as I mentioned, he was destined for much greater things.

Anyway, Ms. Mary was quite the hostess and very often invited people over to her house. I especially liked it when Ms. Mary hosted the prayer meetings. You see, the Christians always took turns going from house to house to pray and enjoy fellowship together. If you asked me, it seemed like Ms. Mary took more than her share of turns. But she didn't seem to mind at all. She just liked people. Anyway, being the young servant girl, I was usually just a bystander and not actively involved in the prayer meeting itself. I was usually around the corner in the next room, in case I was needed for any reason. Oh, how I loved those meetings—even if it did sometimes mean extra work and late hours for me. To hear all of them talk about Jesus and everything he had done was amazing. And then, their prayers! They would pray to God as if he was sitting right there in the room with them! At first I found this all so strange. I especially found it hard to understand how they could pray and worship this

God of theirs when everything seemed to be going wrong.

Interviewer: What exactly was going wrong?

Rhoda: Well, there's this one instance that stands out in my mind so clearly as if it were yesterday.

King Herod was strongly opposed to the Christians and had begun ridiculing and persecuting them. He even went so far as to have the Apostle James killed. That was devastating to the group of believers who met at Ms. Mary's house. I didn't know James very well, but I had met him a couple of times—and even served him once! Everyone was in shock when they got the news about his death. After all, they had been praying for his release since the day he had been arrested. When they learned he had been beheaded, it wasn't long before they all seemed to find their way to Ms. Mary's house. You need to realize, too, that by this time, the Christians had begun to have their prayer meetings secretly and late at night to avoid being seen and harassed.

Anyway, that night after James was killed, I heard the Christians and wondered how they could still worship a God who allowed such things to happen to people who loved him and followed him. But as I listened, I began to realize that their tears weren't just tears of sorrow but also of joy. They were sorrowful that James had suffered such a tragic death and was no longer with them. Yet, they were joyful that he had remained faithful right up to his death and was now present with God. I found it all so strange and hard to understand.

Meanwhile, Herod realized how pleased the Jewish leaders were with his execution of James, so he decided to stay on the attack against the Christians. Then, just after Passover, during the Feast of Unleavened Bread, he arrested Peter and put him in prison.

Interviewer: Why do such a thing during a celebration feast? Why not wait until the feast was over? Or was the timing just by chance?

Rhoda: Oh, it was on purpose, all right. You see, during and just after the Passover, the city was packed with people. To have Peter arrested during such a big event was a strategic move on Herod's part so he could impress the most people. After all, Peter was a high-profile figure among the Christians, so to arrest him was very big news.

Interviewer: Did Herod achieve what he intended by arresting Peter?

Rhoda: Early on, I would have to say he did. The Jews celebrated their "victory," while the Christians became more confused. But what Herod hadn't counted on was the power of prayer. Nor did he realize what a powerful God the Christians worshipped. Actually, I'm not sure the Christians realized it at the time either.

Interviewer: Why do you say that?

Rhoda: Well, from the moment Peter was arrested, Christians began gathering at Ms. Mary's house to pray, just as they had done for James. And I do mean pray. They were so concerned about Peter. Peter was like their leader—the one they looked up to. What would they do if something happened to him? Who would step in and lead them? How could something like this be happening to Peter, of all people? Why would God let this happen? They were so full of questions. They prayed over and over for his safety and protection, as well as for their own. It seems Herod was determined to stop the threat of the Christians by any means possible. They also prayed for Peter to remain faithful, as well as for their own faithfulness. They realized, when facing what appears to be imminent death, many might not be strong enough in their faith to stand firm to the end.

And obviously, they prayed for God to intervene in this time of persecution of all Christians everywhere. But for all their earnestness, it seemed to me they were forgetting a couple of very important things that I'd heard them talk about before. For one thing, they seemed to forget that God's ways are not our ways. And the second was that nothing is impossible with God. I guess their grief over James and their anxiousness and despair over Peter's situation had clouded their minds. Then again, maybe it was Peter who had been the one always doing the reminding. I'm just not sure.

Anyway, the night before Peter's trial, the Christians had gathered once again at Ms. Mary's to pray for Peter—specifically that he would be found innocent and set free the next day. They had been praying for quite some time, and it was getting very late. I was beginning to get so tired. But as long as Ms. Mary had guests in her house, I was expected to be on call. I was fighting the urge to sleep when I heard what I thought was a knock at the door. The others who were praying didn't seem to hear anything, so I thought maybe I had dozed off and dreamed it. Then, I heard it again. I thought, "Now who would be knocking at the door in the middle of the night?" That frightened me. I quickly glanced around the room. Who was missing? As I headed to the door, I couldn't think of anyone Ms. Mary said we should be expecting who wasn't already there. Then I thought, "What if it's Herod's people? What if Herod has found out about the prayer meeting? What if he has sent guards to arrest us?" Then I became really frightened! So, instead of opening the door, I called out. When Peter answered, I recognized his voice immediately. I got so excited that instead of letting him in or even answering him, I ran back upstairs to tell the others.

Interviewer: You mean you didn't even open the door? Rhoda, what were you thinking? Why didn't you at least go ahead and let Peter in?

Rhoda: Well, I guess I was just too surprised and excited to think clearly. Besides, Peter was definitely not who I expected to find at the door. Honestly, he was the about the last person I expected. I guess it just threw me, and I couldn't think straight. After all, it was the middle of the night! And it was Peter, of all people!

Interviewer: I just imagine the Christians were relieved and excited to have their prayers answered so quickly and vividly.

Rhoda: You would have thought so. But actually, they didn't believe me at first! When I interrupted them and told them that Peter was standing at the door, they thought I was crazy. When I kept insisting, they agreed to at least go check. "After all," they said, "maybe it's Peter's angel." I couldn't believe what I was hearing!

Interviewer: What finally convinced them?

Rhoda: Peter himself. He just kept knocking and knocking until finally they opened the door and saw with their very own eyes that it was Peter standing there. Oh, you should have heard the ruckus then! You would have thought they were writing a newspaper article for the Jerusalem Times! They all began questioning Peter at the same time. "Are you really Peter?" "Who let you out?" "What are you doing here?" "When did you make your escape?" "How did you make your escape?" "Where have you been?" "How did you know we'd be here this hour of the night?" Peter immediately cautioned them to quiet down and then motioned to them to let him inside.

Interviewer: You know, throughout history, people have always thought it funny that instead of hurriedly inviting Peter in, you left him standing outside the door. And here the Christians are, with the door wide open, staring Peter in the face, and they do basically the same thing! They left Peter standing outside the door as well. It seems as if there's a lesson here.

Rhoda: What do you mean?

Interviewer: Well, I was thinking about how it is with some people today in modern times when it comes to their relationship with Jesus Christ. He's figuratively standing outside and knocking on their heart's door. And even though the door may be open and they see what they need to do, they are still resistant or hesitant to letting him in. It's almost as if they have to first get all their questions answered before they allow him full access to their hearts.

So, anyway, what happened once Peter got inside the house?

Rhoda: Well, we all went back upstairs, and Peter began telling us his story. We all sat there stunned! We could hardly believe what had happened. And we were all left speechless at what God can do!

Interviewer: Rhoda, what was Peter's story? How did he get out of jail and end up at Mary's house?

Rhoda: We knew that Peter was being watched by armed guards, so that part didn't come as a surprise. But what we didn't know was that a total of 16 guards stood watch over him—four squads of four men each. It seems Herod was making every effort to be sure that there was no chance of his escape! Anyway, that night before his trial, while we had been praying for him, Peter had fallen asleep after being chained between two of the four guards on duty that night. He hadn't been asleep very long when he said he felt a tapping on his side. When he opened his eyes, there was an angel, and the cell was so bright he said he could hardly stand to keep his eyes open, so he squinted as he tried the best he could to figure out what was going on. When he looked around, the guards all appeared to be sound asleep. The bright light hadn't seemed to bother them at all. Then the angel told him to quickly get up and get dressed. As soon as he began to move, the chains that had been around his arms and legs miraculously fell off! Peter got dressed and then followed the angel out of the cell, past two guard posts, and then past the huge iron gate leading to the street. He said it was amazing. He said that everywhere he and the angel went, doors and gates seemed to open and close on their own, and everyone they saw along the way seemed to be sound asleep! Not one of them stirred—even with all the clanging of the gates! At first he said he thought it was all a dream. But then, as they were walking down the street, the angel disappeared. Vanished! All of a sudden there was no bright light, and Peter found himself standing in the middle of the cold, dark street alone. That's when he began to realize that it was all very real—the angel and most importantly, his escape from jail!

Interviewer: So how did he end up at Mary's house?

Rhoda: Well, he said that at first he just stood there, trying to process it all. Actually he found it hard to believe. Then he wondered what to do next. He knew that he couldn't go home. That would be too dangerous. That would be the first place Herod would look for him. That's when he headed to Ms. Mary's house. He said he somehow knew where to go—that Ms. Mary's would be a safe place where he could hide and seek shelter for a while until he figured out what to do.

Interviewer: How long did Peter stay at Mary's house?

Rhoda: Actually, only long enough to tell us the story of his escape. Then, out of the clear blue, it seemed as if he suddenly knew exactly what he should do. He told the Christians who had gathered to make sure all the others knew about what had happened. He seemed to be especially concerned that Jesus' brother, James, be told. I'm not sure why. Maybe it was because Peter could see James' potential and somehow knew that someday he would be a leader in the church in Jerusalem. Or maybe he knew that someday he would write a portion of Scripture that would be passed down through the generations. At any rate, this other James seemed to be on Peter's mind at that moment. Then, just before daylight, Peter left. He didn't say where he was going—probably for our protection as much as his own. He only knew he needed to get out of town.

Interviewer: Rhoda, just being in Peter's presence and hearing firsthand of his escape must have been such a blessing for you.

Rhoda: Oh, it was. It was actually the turning point in my own faith. After seeing with my own eyes and hearing with my own ears how God answers prayer, who wouldn't have believed? So, from that point on, I joined in worship and praise to a God who loves me and who answers prayer.

Interviewer: Rhoda, I hate to do this, but we're going to have to wrap this interview up pretty soon. I wish we had more time to spend with you. But before we let you go, I'd like to ask you to share with us a couple of lessons you learned from your experiences. We're especially interested in anything that might help us improve our walk with Christ today.

Rhoda: Oh, my. You know, I don't think anyone has ever asked me anything like that before! We servant girls weren't usually allowed to express our opinions!

I would have to say that one thing would be to never forget that prayer changes things. Christians need to be people of faith who believe that God does answer the prayers of those who are truly seeking his will. Don't be afraid to pray as often as you can and with as much confidence as you can. And when you pray, believe that you will get an answer. Then, when you get that answer, even though it may not be exactly as you envisioned, try not to act so surprised—be thankful instead!

Then I would also tell you to remember that there are no small tasks in the body of Christ. I mean, look at me for example. Sometimes, like me, what you need to be doing is happening at a time when others are praying or worshipping. Never forget that God knows where you are and what you are doing. Who knows? The place you are serving at the moment might be the place that will give you a firsthand look, or maybe even the first sighting, of a miracle. After all, I was just a servant girl. Yet I was the first one to know that Peter had miraculously escaped from jail.

Then, lastly, I like what you said about people wanting all their questions answered before they let Jesus into their hearts. I'd encourage people today to live more by faith. Once you come to know Jesus and believe that he is God's Son and that he came to save you, go ahead and let Jesus in. Trust him that you will find answers and gain a better understanding later.

Interviewer: Rhoda, thank you so much for joining us and sharing with us this morning. You have certainly left us with a lot to think about. You were truly an amazing young woman who had a once-in-a-lifetime experience. Thank you so much for sharing your story and insights with us.

DISCUSSION QUESTIONS:

1. We hear a lot about living by faith. What exactly is that, and how do you explain that concept to a nonbeliever?

2. Early on, Rhoda says she found it hard to understand how the Christians could continue to pray to and worship their God when everything seemed to be going wrong. As a Christian, how do you handle the difficult times? What keeps you going when everything appears to be falling apart?

3. "God's ways are not our ways" is another saying that you've probably heard more than once. What examples can you give of a way God has worked in your life that was completely different from the way you would have handled things had you been the one in charge?

4. Rhoda mentioned the power of prayer and that perhaps the Christians at Mary's house hadn't realized what a powerful God they worshipped. Can you give some firsthand examples of the power of God?

5. Prayer changes things. What examples can you give of things changed as a direct result of prayer? Can prayer change everything?

6. Rhoda reminds us again of the fact that there are no small tasks in the body of Christ. Let's see how many "behind the scenes" tasks we can think of and how the men and women serving in those areas might be in a position to be the first to witness a miracle.

Ruth

Background Reading: Ruth 1–4
In-Class Reading: Ruth 1:1-2:12; 3:1-4:17
Key Verses: Ruth 1:16-17

Interviewer: Ruth, thank you so much for joining us this morning. For the last several weeks we have had the opportunity to talk with women of Bible times and hear their stories in their own words. And you know, what has amazed us the most is how much we have found that we have in common. However, while we greatly admire you for your loving relationship with your mother-in-law, this is one area most of us feel we fall short. The sad truth is that while we would love to say otherwise, few of us can say we actually love our mother-in-law so much that we would leave family, friends, and country to follow her back to her native homeland. I would say that the question most of us want to know is, "What was your secret?"

Ruth: Boy, that's a good question! You might be surprised to learn that things weren't always rosy between Naomi and me. It's kind of a long story, but at first we were both pretty suspicious of one another. She didn't like it at all when Mahlon and

I became friends. Actually, it wasn't until after her son and I were married that Naomi and I began to slowly develop a friendly relationship. Then, after I became widowed, I came to rely on her and the God she talked about to get me through the heartache. It took some time, but our bond gradually grew to the point of love.

Interviewer: Let's backpedal for just a moment. You said the two of you were suspicious of one another when you first met. Why was that?

Ruth: Well, in a nutshell, it was because we were very different people. She, of course, was older and from Israel; I was younger and from Moab. I'll spare you the long history lesson. Let's just say that during my lifetime, the Moabites and Israelites basically despised each other. So much so, in fact, that it was against their law to have any association with idolatrous Moabites. So, you can just imagine the friction between our families when Mahlon and I were newlyweds.

Interviewer: You know, I hadn't realized there was ever friction between you and Naomi. I guess that means there's hope for the rest of us, isn't there?

Speaking of Mahlon, would you mind telling us a little bit about him? Since the two of you were from different nationalities and cultures and were supposed to stay away from one another, how did the two of you happen to meet?

Ruth: Oh, Mahlon was a kind, loving husband. We met shortly after he and his family moved to Moab. They had traveled there due to a severe famine that was going on in Israel at the time. Under the circumstances, you can imagine how bad the famine must have been for them, as well as several other families, to even consider moving to Moab. Their original plan had been to live there only a short time—only until the famine was over. Then they had planned to head back home.

When Mahlon and I first met, we had an immediate attraction to one another. But neither of our families approved of the arrangement. After all, we worshipped different gods and had grown up in different cultures. But Mahlon and I would not be deterred. I think that's one advantage of youth. Mahlon and I were much more optimistic. Don't get me wrong, we knew there would be struggles along the way, but we knew we could work through them together. When we announced that we wanted to be married, Naomi, Mahlon's mother, was fit to be tied!

Interviewer: I imagine that made for some pretty interesting days early on in your marriage.

Ruth: Did it ever! Then, just when it seemed as if we were beginning to adjust to one another, Elimelech, Naomi's husband and Mahlon's dad, died rather suddenly. That shocked us all. My first instinct was to run to the gods I had grown up with and try to appease them with sacrifices so the curse would be lifted from the family. But Naomi would have none of that. She let me know, in no uncertain terms, that if I was going to be a part of their family, then I was going to be expected to worship just as they did. At first I didn't like being told what I could or couldn't do. And I especially had trouble understanding how

Naomi, Mahlon, and Kilion (Mahlon's brother) could still praise and worship God after such a tragedy.

Oh, they were so patient with me. I shudder to think how differently my life would have been had it not been for them.

Interviewer: What do you mean?

Ruth: Well, at the time, I guess I couldn't see how anything good could ever happen without first offering sacrifices to the gods. Naomi called it pure idolatry and said it was wrong—really, really wrong. Instead, she insisted I worship the "one true God," as she called him. It was all so confusing. But even so, during this time I noticed a big difference in how we mourned. While Naomi was certainly devastated and heartbroken, Elimelech's death did not destroy her. She kept her head up, squared her shoulders, and moved on, doing what needed to be done. She knew and believed that everything was in God's hands and that he would continue to provide for her just as he would continue to love and care for her. I was not so optimistic at first. I had trouble understanding how you worshipped a god you couldn't see or touch. But because I loved Mahlon so much, I was willing to give up my idols in search of Naomi's one true God.

Gradually I came to love the same God Naomi and her sons did. As time passed, we began to settle into a routine and started living as one big, happy family. You know, it wasn't too long after we were married that Kilion also got married. His wife's name was Orpah, and she was a Moabite as I was. The next 10 years or so were wonderful. However, neither Orpah nor I gave birth to children. I think that saddened Naomi. But I did feel as if I had been given a new birth. And I guess in a way, I had. I came to personally know Naomi's one true God. I made a mental decision that I would never, ever go back to idol worship. Oh, how I was tested in the days and years to come.

Interviewer: How so?

Ruth: Well, tragedy struck the family again. And again. Two punches—back to back. That's when both Mahlon and Kilion died. Their deaths really left us spinning. In such a short time we went from being a happy family of five down to three—all women. We weren't sure what we were going to do. Why would God allow this to happen to us? And without a man around, how would we ever be able to provide for ourselves? Back in our day, widowed women were destined to a life of poverty. And to top it all off, Orpah and I had no sons who could grow up to care for us.

Meanwhile, Naomi was in such anguish that she could hardly think straight. After all, she had lost not only her husband but two grown sons as well. And she was still living in a foreign land. She asked a lot of questions of God those first few days and weeks. Things like, "Why did this happen?" "Couldn't one of them have been spared?" "Why them; why not me?" "Am I being punished for coming to Moab in the first place?" "How am I to survive?" But through all her grief, Naomi stuck by God, believing that in the end everything would be OK.

During this time Orpah and I were probably the most tempted to run back home to our families and idol worship. But we didn't! That was such a milestone. Even though we were so new in our faith and had to rely on Naomi to get us through, we—and she—did. We all got through! It wasn't easy by any means, and we spent some long hours talking, crying, and praying. And God was faithful. Then, as soon as Naomi learned that the famine in Israel was over, she decided to head back home. That's when things really began to get interesting!

Interviewer: Dare I ask what kind of things? It seems your life had enough twists and turns already.

Ruth: Well, at first Naomi had decided that the three of us would pack up and head to Bethlehem, the town in Israel where she had come from. But as soon as we got on the road and started on the long journey, Naomi seemed to change her mind. She told Orpah and me to turn around and go back home to our families. We told her that we wouldn't—couldn't—that we were now her family and she was ours and that we wanted to go with her to her homeland. But she insisted. Finally, Orpah was persuaded to return, but I just couldn't. Naomi kept reminding me that she had no more sons for me to marry. And she wasn't sure what, if any, family members remained in Israel who could redeem the family of Elimelech. She wanted to release me so I would be able to marry again within my own nationality. Her thoughtfulness and kindness left me almost overwhelmed. At a time when her life was in such turmoil and uncertainty, her first thoughts were for Orpah and me—that we be free to remarry and go on with our lives and hopefully have children someday. But I had come to love Naomi so much that I couldn't imagine my life without her. Through my tears I mumbled something about going where she would go and dying where she would die and being buried where she would be buried and serving the same God she served.

Interviewer: Ruth, you may not realize this, but those phrases are ones most of us have come to associate with you. Many of us have even used a variation of them in our wedding vows. However, putting all that aside, what were you thinking? Didn't you realize you could possibly remain single and childless the rest of your life or, at the very least, never see your biological family or your friends and homeland again?

Ruth: Yes, I knew that—or at least I think I knew that. I'm not sure it all had soaked in. All I knew at the moment was that I did not want to be separated from Naomi—or God. And I knew that if I went back home, I would lose both. In the few years I had known and been a part of Naomi's family and had come to know God, I was convinced that he was, indeed, the one true God. How thankful I am that Naomi and Mahlon introduced me to him.

Interviewer: So did Naomi allow you to tag along to Bethlehem?

Ruth: Truth be told, I really didn't give her much of a choice! I was clinging to her like you wouldn't believe! It was almost as if I was a little girl hanging onto her mother's apron strings. I wasn't about to let her go! In retrospect, I wonder if maybe this was some sort of test—to see if I loved God only with my mind or if I truly loved him with my whole being—heart, soul, and mind.

Interviewer: What happened after you arrived at your destination?

Ruth: Well, for a while, Naomi was the center of attention. Everyone had heard about her misfortune in losing not only her husband but her sons as well. When she had left Israel years before, she was married and secure. Now, when she returned, she was widowed and poor. Life was not turning out at all the way she had expected. However, Naomi had many old friends who came by and mourned with her. They all felt so sorry for her. I could tell Naomi was loved and well thought of. But early on, it seemed to me as if these friends of hers made an already bad situation worse.

Interviewer: Whatever do you mean by that?

Ruth: Well, her friends showed her such pity that before long she wanted to be called "Mara," which meant "bitter," instead of being referred to by her given name of Naomi, which meant "pleasant." It was almost as if her friends fed her self-pity. And I must say, for a time, "Mara" did seem to fit her better. But I learned that this was all a part of the grieving process Naomi had to go through. Bottom line: Even at her lowest, Naomi still trusted God. Before too long, our situation did begin to improve, and we began to settle into our new life. Then, almost before we knew it, our lives took a drastic and sudden change for the better. God certainly does take care of those he loves.

Interviewer: Yes, we would have to agree that God does, indeed, take care of us—often in very unexpected ways, too. What did God do for you and Naomi to show his love and concern for the two of you?

Ruth: Actually, it all started shortly after we had settled in Bethlehem. The visitors had dwindled down some, and Naomi and I realized that we were going to have to do something or find some way to start providing for ourselves—especially to get some food for the table. That's when I came up with the idea to go and pick up the leftover grain that had fallen to the ground. I knew it would be hot, dirty, and hard work. And I knew that my efforts may or may not give us much food to eat. But it was all I could think to do at the time. And besides, Naomi was too old and frail to be expected to go out and do such work. Our long trip had taken a toll on her physically. I really worried about her. Anyway, Naomi reluctantly agreed, so off I went.

 Now, here is the really neat part! I just "happened" to end up at the field of a man named Boaz who just "happened" to be from the clan of Elimelech— Naomi's husband! I had no idea who he was, and at first, he wasn't sure who I was either! Anyway, after asking some questions, he told me to glean only from his field, to follow along behind the harvesters, and to only glean alongside his servant girls. At the time, I still didn't know who he was—that he was a relative of Naomi's—so it really puzzled me as to why he would be so kind to me and ask such a thing of me. He even told me that whenever I was thirsty to feel free to drink from the water jars his men had already filled.

Interviewer: How or when did you find out who Boaz really was?

Ruth: It wasn't until later that night after I had gone back home to Naomi. When I asked Boaz why he was being so kind to me, he only said that it was because he had heard about me and how I had left my homeland to follow Naomi and live with and take care of her. He then offered me some food, and after I was full, I began to go back to gleaning in the field. I learned later that he had told his workers to "accidentally" drop extra grain for me to gather. Anyway, after I was done gleaning that first day, I ran home to Naomi to show her how much I had gathered in just one day's work.

I wish you could have seen her face! Naomi took one look at the huge amount and asked me where in the world I had gone to get so much. When I told her the man's name was Boaz, Naomi perked up, and a hope began to resurface in her. It was then that I first learned that Boaz was a distant relative. Naomi told me to be sure and do just as he said and to only glean in his field. She told me that since he was a relative, I would be well taken care of. So, that's what I did—every day. Whenever the harvesters were out in the field, I was right there following behind, gathering what was left. Then, every night, I would take back to Naomi all that I had gleaned.

Interviewer: Ruth, that had to have been such a hard life for you. During all this time, did you ever regret your decision to stay with Naomi? Did you ever think about returning to your homeland?

Ruth: Oh, I thought about home a lot—believe me. I really missed my family and friends. But I never regretted what I had done, nor did I ever seriously entertain the idea of going back to Moab. I had come to love Naomi as much as my own mother. There was no way I could just up and leave her. What would have happened to her had I left? Anyway, this was home now. I had no regrets. But I think Naomi did.

Interviewer: What makes you think that?

Ruth: Well, one day Naomi said that it was high time she found a home for me where I would be well taken care of. I assured her that I was being taken care of and that a home with her was all I needed. But evidently she had been bothered by the fact that she had no more sons to give me as a husband. She thought I needed a husband and children and family of my own, so, she began to put the wheels in motion, so to speak, to make that come about.

Interviewer: So what was Naomi's plan?

Ruth: Well, she had been convinced from day one that it was God who had directed my steps to glean in Boaz's field. And as more and more time passed with nothing happening on that front—me finding a husband that is—I guess she decided that it was high time Boaz did his duty as a member of the family and take the initiative to redeem Elimelech's property. You see, it was part of their custom for the nearest family relative to step in as a "kinsman-redeemer" and take responsibility for the family members and property of any man who had died. So, Naomi told me to wash and pour perfume all over me and dress in my finest clothes. Then I was to go to the threshing floor, and after Boaz had finished eating and drinking and had fallen asleep for the night, I was to go uncover his feet and lay down on the ground next to him. Then, when he woke up and found me at his feet, he would know that we wanted to be redeemed—that he could be our kinsman-redeemer and either marry me himself or find someone else to marry me.

Interviewer: Didn't you feel kind of awkward doing this? It sounds as if you were trying to trick Boaz into marrying you.

Ruth: You're right. I was very uncomfortable doing this, but I was so devoted to Naomi. And besides, to be honest with you, deep down, a husband and children were what I wanted also. Naomi had told me that this was their custom and this was what needed to be done. In the end, I trusted her completely and did exactly as she told me, saying exactly what she told me to say.

Interviewer: What was Boaz's reaction when he woke up and found you there?

Ruth: Well, as you can imagine, he was a bit surprised! But he seemed pleased as well. From his comments, I gathered that he had already been thinking along those lines but thought I wouldn't have any interest in him because he was a lot older than me. Anyway, he told me that there was one relative who was closer and who, by law, was to be given first chance to redeem Elimelech's property. He told me to stay the night, and the next morning he would talk with this other man.

Then, the next morning, just before dawn, Boaz loaded me down with grain once again and sent me back home to Naomi.

Interviewer: I'll bet Naomi was on pins and needles to hear how everything went!

Ruth: Oh, you could say that again! She wanted to know absolutely everything. So, I told her exactly what had happened and what Boaz had said he would do. She seemed to relax and told me not to worry, that Boaz was well-known as a man who kept his word, and he undoubtedly would follow through on this matter until it was all settled.

Interviewer: Did he?

Ruth: My goodness, yes! I found out later that he had left shortly after I did to go to the city gate and get this matter taken care of right then. He had wasted no time! As soon as this other relative showed up, and the minute he could get 10 elders together to serve as witnesses, Boaz began explaining the situation to the man—that the property that had belonged to Elimelech had now passed into Naomi's hands, and being the closest relative, he had first chance to redeem it. This man was all set to do so until he learned that I was included in the bargain. Once he found that out, he backed out. I'm not sure if it was because I was a Moabite—a "foreigner"—or if it was the fact that our first son would be able to reclaim the land or if he didn't want to have to share any of his property. Anyway, to make it official, he took off his sandal in front of everyone and gave it to Boaz. Doing that was their way of saying, "It's yours." So that left Boaz the legal heir.

Shortly after that, we were married, and nine months later, we had a son. Oh, you should have seen Naomi's face then! My heart was truly blessed to be able to present her with a grandson. She lived with us and helped care for and rear Obed. And finally, my family was truly complete. Naomi was right—God does take care of those who trust him.

Interviewer: Ruth, it has been such a blessing hearing you tell your story and seeing how God was at work in your life. Before we let you go, however, I'd like to ask you to share with us two or three lessons you learned from your life that we could apply to ours—things that would help us in our daily walk with God.

Ruth: Well, I would, first of all, venture to say that if I had not come to a full understanding of and belief in the one true God, nothing in my life would have been the same. I owe my life to the faithfulness of Naomi, who knew God loved and cared for me—a Moabite girl—even in my ignorance. If you don't do anything else, find God. He already loves you, and he truly can change your life.

Next I would say to not be afraid to obey him. When you feel God is leading you down an uncertain path, trust him. Follow him. Obey him. He can see what lies ahead, and he has only your best interest at heart. I could not imagine a happier ending to my life—wife to Boaz, mother to Obed, daughter to Naomi, accepted among the Israelites, and most importantly, blessed beyond measure by God himself.

Lastly, I would say to remember that God's ways and timing are not the same as ours. Just because you might be able to summarize my life's story in a few short chapters and verses doesn't mean my life's situation changed that quickly. I spent a long time as a widow with a broken heart before God brought me to Boaz. Be patient. It will very often be months or even years before your situation is turned around. Just keep holding on and trusting God. Besides, having or getting everything in an instant is very overrated. Usually, the longer you wait for something, the greater the joy and satisfaction when you get it.

Interviewer: Well summarized. Ruth, thank you for taking the time to join us and for sharing your life story with us. You have been quite a blessing. Thank you so much.

DISCUSSION QUESTIONS:

1. It has been said that "friendship weaves lives together." That was certainly the case with Naomi and Ruth. Many women today struggle with their mother-in-law relationship and most certainly don't develop a true friendship as Naomi and Ruth did. What may have caused Ruth and Naomi to develop harmony instead of friction?

2. Naomi allowed Ruth to see firsthand her developing relationship with God—all the hurts, sorrows, tears, and anger, as well as the times of joy and blessings. When you're going through an especially difficult time, how inclined are you to feel that your thoughts and questions about God or your anger towards him should be kept from everyone—even your best friends? Why?

3. What makes Ruth's declaration of love and loyalty for Naomi such an ideal example of pure and unselfish devotion?

4. Naomi's plan to get Ruth a husband may have seemed strange to Ruth. Yet, she did exactly as she had been told, trusting Naomi's experience and knowledge. What do you think may have happened if Ruth had refused to follow Naomi's advice and done things her own way? How important is it for us to listen to and follow the advice of Christian parents or older role models? Why?

5. In Ruth's story, we learn that Boaz had an outstanding reputation and had proven to be a man who could be counted on. What does it take to develop a good repu-

tation, and what can be done if a person's reputation is less than stellar?

6. Ruth advises us to be patient and allow God time to work in our lives. In our microwave world, how hard is it to stop or even slow down to wait on God? What things should we be doing as we wait?

Leader's Guide for Small Groups

*W*hat Were You Thinking? is an ideal short study for any women's small group. This study is an attempt to bring more than a dozen Bible-time women to life by looking not only at their circumstances and experiences but at their emotions as well. It is my desire that we 21st-century women will come to realize that the emotions of women living more than 2,000 years ago were very similar to those we experience today. And I think we may be amazed to discover that given similar situations, we would react in much the same way as did our Bible-time examples.

If you are the leader of a group study of this book, allow me to share some thoughts on ways to make your study successful. My first suggestions would be to bathe the study and preparations in prayer. Pray that God would prepare the hearts of those who will be attending your small group. Pray, too, that their eyes will be opened wide so they can see the lives of these Bible-time women in vivid, living color and not just in black and white.

Next, I would recommend that you plan to study one lesson per week. There are thirteen lessons, making this ideal for a quarterly study. Since each lesson is self-contained, this study is also ideal for groups where women need to miss occasionally due to other commitments.

Note that for each woman featured, there is a Background Reading, an In-Class Reading segment, and a Key Verse (or verses). It is my suggestion that you ask the women to read the Background Reading during the week preceding each interview. In that way, they are somewhat familiar with the woman being featured that week. Then, ask for a volunteer from the group to read the In-Class Reading to introduce the lesson, followed by a second volunteer to read the Key Verse(s). By this time, the women in your group should be familiar with the featured woman, and she will seem more like a friend you're eager to visit with.

I suggest treating the lesson portion itself as if it was an actual interview. I also recommend that you read ahead to determine who might make a good "Eve" or "Abigail," and so forth. I think as you read through these interviews, you will be able to recognize personalities that match the personalities of women you know or who are in your small group. For instance, you probably wouldn't want to ask someone extremely outgoing to be Hannah or Mary but rather someone more naturally quiet and reserved. Instead, enlist the more outgoing personalities to portray women like Abigail, Sapphira, or Martha. The more closely matched the personalities are, the better your interviews will be.

If possible, rearrange furniture so the interviewer and interviewee are at an angle facing one another and not side-by-side. Try to know the contents of the script well enough that you're not constantly reading it. Eye contact with each other as well as others in the small group is important. Also, choosing to have the woman being interviewed dress up in a robe and/or scarf is another good idea. Use your imagination. Do everything you can to help the Bible-time women jump off the pages of Scripture and into the hearts of the women in your small group.

Following each lesson are six discussion questions. Not every woman will be able to answer every question, but do try to include everyone at some point in the discussion time each week. If you have someone new to the group, consider asking her to be one of your readers. In that way she will have the opportunity to participate in class in a non-threatening manner.

Finally, have fun! The study of Scripture should be exciting. Keep the atmosphere in your group relaxed and casual. Enjoy the opportunity to get to better know not only these Bible-time women but your own modern-day women as well.

Precious leader, thank you for being available and open to using your God-given strengths and abilities in facilitating this study. Continue to prayerfully seek God's guidance and wisdom as you lead. Pray also for your ears to be fine-tuned during the discussion times in order that you may hear any special, heartfelt needs of the women participating in this study. Thank you for being God's vessel. May God richly bless you.

LaVergne, TN USA
10 June 2010
185766LV00001B/138/P